Every English Teacher

A guide to English teaching
for the non-specialist

Anthony Adams and **John Pearce**

Oxford University Press 1974

Oxford University Press, Ely House, London W.I

Glasgow New York Toronto Melbourne Wellington
Cape Town Ibadan Nairobi Dar es Salaam Lusaka
Addis Ababa Delhi Bombay Calcutta Madras Karachi
Lahore Dacca Kuala Lumpur Singapore Hong Kong
Tokyo

We make grateful acknowledgement to McGibbon
& Kee and Harcourt Brace Jovanovich, Inc. for
permission to reprint 'anyone lived in a pretty
how town' by e.e. cummings from *Complete Poems*
1913–1962 copyright 1940 by e.e. cummings;
copyright 1968 by Marion Morehouse Cummings;
and to David Higham Associates Ltd. for
John Heath-Stubbs' 'The History of the Flood'.

Printed in Great Britain
by J. W. Arrowsmith Ltd., Bristol.

Contents

Preface

'Every teacher in English is a teacher of English.' This remark first appeared in the Newbolt Report on 'The Teaching of English in England', published by the Board of Education in 1921. Like most epigrams it is a half-truth. The true part of it is that teachers by their example may instruct more powerfully than by their lessons; and the way they use English will influence all their pupils. The untrue part of it is the notion that anyone who can speak English can also, by virtue of that fact, teach it.

We believe that there are large numbers of teachers engaged in English teaching who are baffled by the conflicting ideologies that occupy the minds of some specialists in English, and who want practical guidance about what to do. We have tried to provide this guidance by a combination of principles and examples, so that the reader will be able to use the principles to work out further examples for himself.

The main conflict among English teachers in recent years has concerned the relationship between language and literature. Without pretending that we have effected a finally adequate reconciliation of the claims of literature with those of the linguistically-orientated approach, we have tried to offer a synthesis which will make practical sense. The general pattern of English teaching has undergone a great deal of change in the last twenty years or so, and such change will continue. Many books about the subject have been written in that time, some of them from embattled positions, and it is not our intention to add to that long debate. Rather, we have tried to make a straightforward guide to the best of current thought and practice.

We have focused on the teaching of mixed-ability classes in the age range from 9 to 13. This reflects the area of greatest need, since it is the age range in which the most formative changes in the language competence of children occur, and where the greatest opportunities for a major improvement of classroom practice exist.

We wish to thank Norman Newhouse, Sylvia Stephenson, and other colleagues for their care in reading large parts of the manuscript and helping us to remove some of its defects. We are grateful, too, for discussions over many years with colleagues and friends in the National Association for the Teaching of English, and especially to its former Chairman, W.H. Mittins, who encouraged the first proposal for a guide of this kind. The errors which remain, like the opinions we express, are the sole responsibility of the authors.

Anthony Adams
John Pearce

Chapter 1

The tradition of English teaching

For a number of years there has been a scarcity of English teachers with specialist qualifications in the subject. Quite apart from official figures which may be available, this has been obvious to head teachers and administrators. There is a difference between a shortage of English teachers and a scarcity of specialists in subjects like French or Mathematics. The teacher who knows little French cannot teach it; and likewise with mathematics. But many teachers are expected to teach English, and to be able to do so, simply by virtue of being speakers of the language. This may not always be a bad thing. Indeed, we have seen many cases where it has been an excellent thing. But it does mean that schools can ask members of staff to 'do a little English' without inquiring too closely into the teachers' state of readiness for the work. One consequence has been a stream of inquiries about how English should be taught.

A very pressing reason for trying to give these queries a coherent answer is that English teachers, within their own specialism, have become notorious for the length and acrimony of their arguments about aims and methods. Most secondary teachers know that there are enthusiasts for creative writing here, believers in literary experience there, advocates of 'basics' somewhere else. To those not involved in the arguments between these ideas their supporters appear to be in collision with one another, often fundamentally. Most of these debates, however, are to our mind relatively marginal. We shall be concerned to identify and describe an approach to English teaching with which most specialist English teachers, whatever their individual emphasis, would feel generally happy. In order to do this, we shall try first to describe the pattern of thought and practice out of which many of these dissenting voices sprang, and which remains, for most others who have stayed at school to 18, the basis of their thinking about the subject. This pattern was adequate in its time but is not adequate today; and it is not difficult to understand why.

First, however, we would like to emphasize that 'non-specialist', as we use it, is a descriptive term and in no sense a critical one. There are many English teachers who, having trained in other subject fields, took up work in English for the love of it and became outstanding specialists in it. The number of teachers who make this kind of shift between fields appears to be growing, which is all to the good, and we would hope that those thinking of moving towards English may find these pages useful. In secondary schools, also, many English departments are led by a single specialist, with a team made up from portions of the time of a whole series of specialists in several other subjects. Again, there are many teachers of middle school and older junior school classes, who have to cater for almost all of their pupils' work in the ordinary curriculum, but feel that their work in English lacks the zest, the technique, or indeed the effectiveness of their work in mathematics. Many students in colleges of education have a pattern of studies which includes a very attentuated 'method' course in English, and find that it does not prepare them adequately for so vital an element in the curriculum they have to teach. We believe that all these kinds of teacher, and others, will welcome practical help offered in a principled fashion. That is, our examples are grounded in a rationale from which teachers can work out further examples for themselves; and we have tried to make our principles explicit, rather than leave them to be inferred from the examples. Taken together, the very diverse kinds of teacher we have mentioned add up to a considerable influence in the educational system. At a time when there is wide public and professional concern about English teaching we feel that they should receive more recognition, that the difficulty of successful work in English should be appreciated, and that they should be given the support of up-to-date knowledge.

One may well ask what the whole body of non-specialist English teachers might have in common, so far as it affects their conception of the subject and the proper way to teach it. In many matters of detail, probably, the answer would have to be that they have very little. A majority of them, however, and certainly the vast majority of those over 25, have shared a common experience of English at a formative stage of their own educational careers: they have been candidates, usually successful, for the Ordinary Level of the General Certificate of Education, and their subjects have included English Language and, often, English Literature. Crucially important examinations are memorable to all of us, and it would be surprising if most people who have taken the G.C.E. in a subject successfully did not feel that their work for it was concerned with the essentials of the subject. The approach to English that was implied by the way it was examined in the G.C.E. until very recently was a very strong influence on the earlier work of those who took the subject. In giving an account of the approach to English which led to the G.C.E., therefore, we shall make some unavoidable generalizations in order to identify the main features of it.

Quite the most distinctive feature of G.C.E. English work, however, until a little over a decade ago, was that it was largely confined to grammar and public schools. Many of the pupils in these schools came from backgrounds which were linguistically privileged or very ambitious for their children. For many pupils, the English curriculum in those schools could take for granted, and could rely on, a degree of linguistic competence in the pupils which the comprehensive school of today finds itself having to create. The teaching which resulted could make a number of assumptions which no longer hold. Our thesis is that the model of English teaching which was a formative experience for most of today's teachers cannot be expected to work in today's classrooms. This is not necessarily a criticism of O-Level itself. Rather, it is a criticism of applying to a quite new situation the assumptions and practices which were well adapted to a quite different one. While this gradual change was taking place, and before it was possible to see it in perspective, there grew up considerable criticism of G.C.E. approaches to English (such as Brian Jackson's *English Versus Examinations*, Chatto and Windus), and the O-Level examination papers now set by most examining boards incorporate many of the improvements sought by these critics. But this area of debate has been a rather specialist concern, and may be quite unknown to the non-specialist, so that for the latter the enduring influence may well be the pattern as he experienced it before these changes.

Language and literature

The G.C.E. inherited from the older School Certificate the practice of treating English language and English literature as separate 'subjects'. It also inherited the division of 'language' into 'component parts' usually known as 'essay', 'summary', 'comprehension', and 'grammar and usage'. To a greater or lesser degree, the generations of textbooks published for preparing candidates for English adopted these divisions, and generations of teachers followed them without serious question. As we shall see in Chapter 9, there were dissenting voices as early as 1917, but it was not

until 1965 that the form of the examination began to change to any
significant extent. The way in which historical change could cause an
examination to become out of step with its clientele and its original
intentions is well illustrated by the case of English Literature. It settled
very early into the procedure of questioning candidates very closely on a
small number of prescribed books, usually three at Ordinary Level. The
assumption was at the time that the three books would be representative
of, and only a small part of, the wider reading naturally pursued by the
candidate. However, as the population of secondary schools grew, and in
time expanded out of all recognition, what happened in practice was that
most candidates concentrated on the set books to the exclusion of all
else. What originated as a sampling developed into a memory-grind, and
the enormous increase in numbers taking the Ordinary Level examinations
in the 1950s and 1960s accentuated the difficulty of bringing about
improvements[1]. There are now many more choices of syllabus and of
approach available in O-Level both in English language and in English
literature. The Certificate of Secondary Education (C.S.E.) has treated
language and literature as parts of a single subject. Sustained efforts
are now taking place to bring about a Common Examination at 16+, and
the problem of reconciling this difference in approach is a good example
of the difficulties which these negotiations will have to overcome.

Language

'Essay'

In the past the ability to write a particular kind of prose at some length
was regarded as one of the acid tests of the 'educated' man. Such prose
was conceived as being addressed to a public audience, impersonal in
expression, formal in style, without topical or very local allusion, and free
from literary adornment and from colloquialism alike. This kind of prose
was normally referred to as 'essay' writing or 'composition'. Its justification was usually held to be linked with the future demands of academic
life. For those who are to pursue scholarly studies that justification may
still apply, but the point of entry to higher education has moved from
16 to 18, so weakening the case for a test of this kind at 16. Moreover,
outside university work, 'essay' prose is almost never expected of adults
unless they are professional writers. Most adolescents and adults only
write at length if they have a compelling motive. Even when they do write,
they are usually free to use the first person, and to ignore several other
restrictions which used to be part of the conventions of 'essay'. The need

for a motive is especially pressing in the case of children, and the lack of one is evident in the oft-heard cry of 'Please, sir, I can't think of anything to say.'

Teachers who found themselves faced with this response to classroom writing-tasks in most or all of their classes, as they usually did in secondary-modern schools, were led to experiment with much less rigid frameworks. They discovered the potential of using stimuli for imaginative forms of expression. They saw the value of free verse as a medium for their pupils. They felt their way to abandoning altogether the conventional norms of seriousness and length which pervaded 'composition' in schools a generation ago. And they found that in the long run the pupil who as a third- or fourth-former did a great deal of committed or engaged imaginative writing was, in his O-Level year, a much better writer.

The argument from higher education, which we have mentioned as one justification for 'essay', was for many years supported by the argument from marking. This held that imaginative writing was impossible to mark fairly, and hence that the really serious writing, that done for examinations, should exclude it. The argument has crumbled with remarkable speed in recent years, chiefly through the influence of research at the London Institute of Education. Professor J.N. Britton and his colleagues carried out a study ('Multiple Marking of English Composition', *Examinations Bulletin No. 12*, H.M.S.O.) which has affected everyday practice a great deal. It showed that a panel of two or three examiners, using a basis of rapid 'impression' marking, could mark O-Level compositions more reliably and more fairly than a single examiner working alone with a detailed mark-scheme. Most of the G.C.E. examining boards have adopted multiple marking to some extent, and the greater freedom which it brings to the examiners who set the question papers is already evident. In particular, the frigid formality with which question papers used to address the candidate is disappearing, and the traditional one-word subject has been replaced by more constructive guidance. Here, as in other respects, the formative experience of English which many future teachers are now having at 16 is much more diverse than it was.

The London Institute's research also explored the responses to differing kinds of writing task. The discussion of abstract topics or ideas brought relatively less successful writing, even from able candidates, but the use of imaginative stimuli such as music or poems led to significantly better writing. The tasks which the candidates found more enjoyable also appear to have brought a better performance in respect of mechanical accuracy.

Comprehension

One of us recently heard a student describing a former teacher:

> She used to bring in a duplicated sheet with a poem or a piece of prose
> on it. We would usually read it through and find it quite beyond us.
> Then she would start digging away at it with us. She almost never *told*
> us anything: just asked questions, and we had to work it all our for
> ourselves, out loud. Nine times out of ten what we dug up would be
> fascinating. Even if we had read a piece before, we found all sorts of
> new things there. She was wonderful at asking the question you never
> thought of, and she always seemed as fascinated as we were.

Interestingly, the teacher described here was a geographer who liked 'to
do a bit of English for fun'. Many English teachers would feel honoured
by such a description, and it is an admirable account of what comprehension is really about: the close study of meanings in written texts. It works
by exercising a gentle pressure to bring about in the pupil a more accurate,
perceptive, and complex response to language. It has two long-term aims.
One is to bring the pupil to view himself, when he is engaged as a reader,
as capable of perceiving much more in a text than he can hope to see at
first glance. The other is to bring about the realization that the ensuing
effort of closer study and perception is rewarding and enjoyable.

In this sense, comprehension work is to some extent an open-ended
procedure: the response of a class to a text should not be predetermined.
But for all its difficulty, the process of mutual engagement in exploring a
piece of written language is of central importance in English teaching, at
every level of age and ability. The reason for this is clear: language is not
simple. (Literature would be very dull if it were.) In particular, language
is not just a linear sequence of discrete chunks of meaning. Any attempt
to put meaning into language entails allowing for the echoes set up by
the language used just before, whether we are merely conversing with
friends or operating in a wider context. For example, the words of the
Book of Common Prayer are being exploited as well as alluded to in
Shakespeare's

> Let me not to the marriage of true minds
> Admit impediments.

In the same way, the weight given in our minds to the last consonant of
'admit' is increased by its near-echo of 'Let' and 'not' in the previous
line. In any literary text, whether prose or verse, novel or play, the
meaning of any one item is more than its dictionary definition. Un-
covering this complex web of interconnection between the parts of a

work is an integral element in 'comprehension' work.

The treatment of 'comprehension' in examinations and their preparatory textbooks may seem a far cry from what we have just described. We
find passages of prose, usually non-fictional, with sets of words and
phrases picked out, and invitations to say what they mean 'in your own
words'. This approach to comprehension usually takes it for granted that
the exercise is to be a written one. The mutual exploration of meanings
which is the heart of real comprehension work depends vitally, in our
view, on being done orally. The use of a written procedure inevitably
brought about a profound change in the activity taking place: response and
exploration were replaced by vocabulary-hunting and a search for right
answers. The change was so great that the activity which became conventional under the heading of comprehension urgently needed a justification.
The one most commonly offered was that it extended the pupils'
vocabulary, and the younger the pupils involved the more firmly this
defence was adopted.

We can be quite certain that the amount of additional vocabulary which
children learn, in the sense of acquiring additional working vocabulary,
from comprehension exercises, is infinitesimal. If a pupil does a
'comprehension exercise' once a week for a school year, and does each of
them carefully, he will perhaps encounter thirty words which he has not
met before and as many again which are only dimly familiar. In the nature
of the case he is unlikely to remember and subsequently use more than a fifth
of these. As a way of acquiring a dozen new words a year, comprehension
exercises are laughably laborious. This is, quite simply, an inefficient way
of doing that particular job, which is far better done by helping children
to become enthusiastic readers and eager talkers, with challenging writing
tasks and free access to dictionary and reference book. The trust which
has been placed in comprehension exercises rests on confusing children's
recognition vocabulary with their facility in providing synonyms and
paraphrases.

It will be objected, of course, that the teacher has a duty, with many
children of 9 to 13, to 'give them language'. But normal children over
the age of 9 cannot be described as 'not having language'. Rather, they
appear to be in this condition because they are constrained in some way
to speak less freely than they are able. Children very frequently do not
produce the language a teacher is looking for in the setting where it is
expected, but that is a quite different matter. It cannot be stressed too
often that English teaching needs to start, not with efforts to 'give them
language', but with a search for ways of getting children to give us the

language they already have. There is nothing odd, for adults or children, in being tongue-tied in one setting and fluent in another, but it is misleading, and may be dangerous, to equate a child's linguistic capacity with his performance in school.

Summarizing

The importance of 'précis' or 'summary' in the formal English work of secondary schools has declined dramatically in recent years. Some of the G.C.E. boards now say in their O-Level English syllabuses that it may not occur in question papers at all, and when it does appear it is in a much less formalized way than in the past. This decline corresponds closely to the movement of specialist opinion, which has come to regard summarizing as not particularly valuable, or even particularly reliable as an examining device. Certainly there is no need whatever to include summarizing, or exercises designed to lead towards it, at any time before the fourth year of the secondary course. This position is in marked contrast to that of less than twenty years ago, when summary was felt to be a difficult exercise needing long preparation. For this reason, exercises in it appeared in the second-year sections, and even in some first-year sections, of course books. Many course books dating from that period are still in use in schools, and such exercises as may occur in them up to the third year of secondary work should be ignored. This illustrates both the tendency of O-Level approaches to assert themselves further and further down the curriculum, and the unfortunate effects of using course-books which have become out of date.

Grammar and usage

The typical Ordinary Level paper in English Language in the 1950s awarded 40% of the marks for the essay, 25% for the comprehension, 20% or 25% for the summary, and the balance for a question in the area called 'grammar and usage'. Because many who have succeeded in their educational careers were taught some kind of grammar during those careers, they believe that lessons in clause analysis or the parts of speech were of direct value in helping them to speak or write better English. This is a perfectly natural viewpoint, but it has been put to the test of research on a fairly sophisticated basis and has been found quite without foundation. (For a summary, see Andrew Wilkinson's *The Foundations of Language*, O.U.P., pp. 32–5.) Many teachers will find such a conclusion difficult to accept, until they appreciate that what applies to grammatical knowledge in learning a foreign language does not apply at all in one's own language.

Moreover, the use of questions about grammar was firmly rejected by an official committee of high professional standing in 1965, and has been almost entirely abandoned in G.C.E. examinations. (Eighth Report of Secondary Schools Examination Council, *The Examining of English Language*; H.M.S.O.)

English teaching in the past decade or so has accordingly given up teaching the formal nomenclature of grammar as well as the procedure of analysis which used it. Many teachers regard this as throwing the baby out with the bath-water, believing that the names of the parts of speech are part of the common cultural stock, however sadly misunderstood they may often be. There are circumstances where it may be genuinely useful to know what a noun is, and where a child who does not know is placed at a disadvantage. The same may well apply, at the middle-secondary stage, to such concepts as tense or clause. An English department, and in a small school the whole staff, should attempt to reach agreement about what terms it is going to teach and when. But it should be done on the clear understanding that nobody expects such knowledge to have much effect on how well the pupils use language.

The distinction between grammar and usage is more complicated. Academic specialists in the study of language, that is to say scholars in the field of general linguistics, are unanimous in reserving the term 'grammar' for the *descriptive* study of how language and its users *do* behave. The general run of people view 'grammar' as *prescriptive*, i.e. as setting forth how the language *ought* to be used. Considerations of correctness, however, really should be treated as questions of usage. One reason is that 'bad grammar', strictly speaking, exists only in unmeaningful sentences, which normal native speakers of a language do not produce. A more serious reason is that matters of correctness are subject to the inexorable fact that language changes. For example, the prestige of standard English accents is much less than it was a generation ago; the distinction between 'will' and 'shall' has virtually disappeared; within another decade or so, the notion that there is anything dubious about 'different to' or 'different than' will have been forgotten; and the old taboo has almost gone that it is naughty to occasionally split an infinitive. There are many who feel personally threatened by linguistic change of this kind. This is because their own education forged a deep-seated bond between their sense of their own identity (as, among other things, 'educated' people) and their adoption of certain patterns of linguistic usage. Since we now live in a very different kind of society, we do not benefit the children of this generation by creating a new intolerance of the same kind.

The close connection between usage and social rather than linguistic distinctions in England has created a ready market for manuals like Gowers' *The Complete Plain Words* (Penguin). As guides for the uncertain, these have some value, but they have limitations. Like some dictionaries, many of them reinforce the idea that spoken usage, under the pejorative label 'colloquial', is bad. Hence, they imply that written English is better than spoken, instead of merely different. For reasons to be explored in later chapters, the spoken language of children between 9 and 13 is one of the English teacher's most valuable resources, and should not be discountenanced unless it is actually offensive[2]. In any case, many English teachers think it is disproportionate to spend time getting the pupils hung up over errors which will drop out of use as they mature. A community which is no longer worried about *undoubtably* is also unlikely to be disturbed by *get hung up over*. There is a place, of course, for sustained exploration of verbal contrasts which depend on a single syllable, especially in that important area of the lexicon that relies on prefixes and suffixes, but this is best done as an exploration into the resources of the language rather than as a process of picking one's way between right and wrong. The underlying processes of affixation in English are remarkably regular, but even here the constant invention of new terms provides more evidence of the weight of linguistic change, and hence of the absurdity of laying down rigid rules of usage[3].

Literature

Class readers and set books

One of the underlying assumptions of the English curriculum which derived from O-Level was that it could be taught in lessons where a whole class did the same thing at the same time with much the same outcome. The coming of the mixed-ability class has overturned this assumption. It seems that a high proportion of comprehensive schools have moved from streaming their initial intake and have opted firmly for mixed-ability grouping for at least the first year. Where certain key subjects can be 'setted' into ability groups, mixed-ability classes continue for English and other subjects well beyond the first year. If the component parts of the old approach to language work prove impracticable in such a setting, those of literature work do so even more clearly. The class reader, once a staple of classroom English, is a case in point. It was usually a prose book and often a classic novel. Parts of it might be read aloud by the teacher, but most would be handled by 'reading round the class'. This procedure often enabled the teacher to secure close attention by making unpredictable changes of the pupil doing the reading. In this way a teacher would secure very close attention—to himself rather than to the text. As a way of involving children in literature it proved cumbersome, since those who were interested read ahead and the rest were often bored. In other settings the class reader was apt to be rationalized as a way of improving the pupil's reading ability. The experienced teacher of juniors, of course, will see at once that it is an inefficient way of helping a child who is behind in reading, since the use of the whole class as an audience increases anxiety. The need in such cases is for individual attention or work in very small groups.

The contradictions of trying to use class readers with mixed-ability groups can be resolved in many ways, ranging from the individual's self-chosen book from a class or school library to the use of reading-groups where each member of a group has a copy of the same book and there are work-cards and instructions which enforce a careful reading of it. The solution to be adopted has to be chosen in the light of the particular conditions, bearing in mind that children read more, and read it more profitably, if they are reading books that they enjoy. The practice of setting children free to choose their own in-school reading, and equipping school libraries to cater for this demand, has greatly improved ordinary English teaching. Such a change entails restoring some element of close reading, and making provision, where necessary, for individual children to be heard reading aloud by an adult. We deal with several aspects of this matter in later chapters.

The study of 'set books' derived from the syllabuses of English literature examinations, and often led to similar treatment of class-readers with younger pupils. This often took the form of context questions, where a short extract (usually known as a 'gobbet') was quoted, for the pupil to 'place' in its fuller context and comment on. For the candidates for O-Level English literature the unpredictability of gobbets remains an anxiety, but many question papers have changed in recent years to a more open approach. A gobbet approach to class-readers with pupils under the age of 15 is quite inappropriate: if a text is imaginative literature in prose or verse, it calls primarily for an imaginative response, in talk or drama or writing.

Poetry and plays

We mention these elements very briefly because they have been more open to change over a longer period than other areas of English teaching. Many teachers needed little persuading that a class sitting passively reading out the lines of a play was not grasping more than a fraction of its significance.

The proponents of drama in education are far from unanimous about how
work in improvization should be linked up with the study of written plays,
but the question is widely discussed. To a lesser extent poetry in the classroom has also moved from a passive study of other people's writing to an
active, creative engagement in poetic expression. It is again true that the
condition of the stock cupboard has all too often been a brake on progress;
however, the use of free verse as a medium for children's writing has been
supported by most of those who have written since 1950 on the teaching
of English, and its effectiveness with a wide range of ability has fully
justified it.

Course books

In its most rigid form, traditional English went further than dividing
the subject into separate components. It often provided each component
with its own textbook and gave each class a separate weekly period for it.
Pressures of cost and convenience, however, naturally led to the writing
of series of textbooks which sought to bring the main components within
a single book, with one volume for each school year. Not surprisingly,
such course books prospered, especially in the rapid expansion of
secondary education which followed the 1944 Education Act. However,
the majority of English specialists have in practice relied on them for a
short period at the beginning of their careers, only to outgrow them. This
is because the course book normally sets finite goals and causes a
fragmentation of what the teacher would like to see treated with coherence.
The exercises which are the basic material of course books predetermine
the outcomes of class work which the teacher would often prefer to keep
open-ended, and are often based exclusively on written sources. Another
reason for the failure of the course book in England has been the natural
desire of publishers to cater for many different markets in a single
publication. These have usually included English-speaking schools in
Africa and many other parts of the world, whose needs are quite different
from those of the domestic market. Secondary course books may be a
useful support when no other help is available; and that is a situation
which is still regrettable, however common it may be.

The emergence of full-scale curriculum development projects in recent
years has also thrown into doubt the value of course books written by
individual teachers, since project materials draw upon a much wider range
of knowledge and experience, and are often subject to some degree of
testing and evaluation. Perhaps fortunately, no project has been set up to

product anything like a course book for English. Many publishers, however, have begun to take much closer cognizance of the views and practices of English specialists, and have issued collections of materials which break free from the established course book pattern[4].

The position of course books in secondary school English is thus weakening considerably. The same can hardly be said about course books written for use in primary schools. These take two forms: series of text-books, and series of workbooks. The textbook form is open to precisely the same objection as the secondary kind, with the additional problem that they contain information about language, and especially about 'correct grammar', which is both quite unnecessary and in many respects inaccurate. In particular, course books for primary schools show no awareness, for the most part, of the wide differences between spoken and written language.

In workbook form, textbooks in English for primary schools rely on exercises which ask children to put single words into ready-made slots. Such work may reinforce reading, but it offers no instruction whatever. It keeps children superficially busy while the teacher attends to more urgent needs. The pacing, timing, and linguistic content of most such workbook series are often extraordinary. The amount of vocabulary which an able child would gain from them is no greater than would be gained by formal comprehension exercises at a later stage, and for average children the gain would be even smaller. The same amount of time devoted to reading children's novels of reasonable quality, or to talking with a sympathetic adult, would do infinitely more good.

Conclusion

The approach to English which relies on a sharp division between literature and language, and between the component parts of the latter, breaks down in the classrooms of today. This fact reflects both the unsatisfactory analysis of linguistic realities lying behind such divisions and their origin in a set of test procedures. The realities of English are no longer met by using 'component parts'. Literature can only exist in the medium of language. Language is powerful when people make it their servant rather than their master. When they go further to make language express complex meanings in complex ways, they are on the way to making literature as well as to exercising control over an otherwise inchoate experience of life. Beyond this, too, children of any age need the contribution that only literature can make to their education. For it extends their horizons, challenges their minds, stirs their feelings—and it does these things with words. Because literature cannot exist without language, and language without literature is less than humane, the alleged competition between language-centred and literature-centred approaches to English is for us a sterile distraction.

Chapter 2

The foundations of English teaching

The traditional approach to English is in many ways like the traditional approach to other subjects in supposing that the subject can be divided up into components. But it is not only in its indivisible quality that English differs from other subjects. For as well as being an element in the curriculum, English provides the medium of instruction for all the others. Moreover, many of the other school subjects derive from academic disciplines which provide an obvious structure for the planning of school instruction, and which specify a body of knowledge to be imparted. History deals with a body of historical events, and the time scale itself points to a structure for syllabuses. Pupils can thus be asked to study the evolution of present-day institutions, or the growth of civilizations from their earliest times. Such structures may be crudely over-simplified, but their relationship to the underlying scholarly discipline is plain.

In fact, of course, most subjects taught in school are undergoing a process of rethinking. The relationship between school subject and scholarly discipline is in question all over the map of knowledge, and the complex process by which society defines and distinguishes between disciplines is itself now coming under intense scrutiny.[1] The sense of crumbling boundaries between once clearly distinct subjects is affecting many teachers who are dissatisfied with the traditional subject disciplines as a basis for the school curriculum. Partly the discontent reflects the difficulty of finding room in the timetable for adequate representation of each subject. It also reflects a growing awareness that traditional subjects can only be taught as separate subjects at the price of forcing pupils into an excessive and premature specialization. The English teacher is particularly strongly affected by this prevailing unease. Nobody questions the decisive importance of the competence which English teachers exist to produce in their pupils—on the contrary the demand for it is stronger than ever. But the scholarly disciplines of English, as they are sustained in universities and colleges of education, lay emphasis on literary criticism and scholarship, or on linguistic theory

and analysis, studies which have a very tenuous connection with English
lessons in the middle school. The widespread debate about English teaching reflects a basic uncertainty about what the English teacher should
teach and what his pupils should learn in the classroom.

At the same time the pupils who face the English teacher have become
sharply more diverse than they were. The increased numbers of immigrant
pupils, the diversification of junior school work brought about by the pro-
gressive removal of the 11+ selection procedure, and the steady decline
of deferential respect for middle class ways of speaking are only the
most obvious factors at work. In these circumstances some teachers
have taken refuge in a version of traditional English teaching which is
distressingly superficial and inert. There has been some reversion to approaches which employ a cumulative, step-by-step pattern of learning. For
example, many junior school pupils are taught information about nouns
and verbs, so that they can write simple sentences. They go on to adjectives,
adverbs, prepositions, conjunctions, each in turn attended with exercises
and tests, and the assumption appears to be that at the end of the process
the pupils will know how to write sentences which use these parts of
speech because they know what the parts of speech are. In the same way,
at a higher level, A.F. Scott's well-used *From Paragraph to Essay* (C.U.P.)
suggests that the secondary school pupil can move from practice with the
simple sentence, through mastery of the complex sentence, into control
of the paragraph, and beyond it to joining paragraphs together to form
essays. There is an appealing simplicity about these approaches. The truth
is that language skills do not accumulate in this simple fashion, and cannot
be made to do so in the classroom. One of the reasons is that the description of language underlying such approaches is naively over-simplified, and
in some respects downright incorrect, but the main reason is that language
learning does not take place in this fashion. If many pupils in the past who
had this kind of instruction did ultimately learn to write good prose, it was
not by virtue of this kind of English teaching.

The same holds for the model of English teaching which lays emphasis
on knowing biographical and other information about great writers, or
historical fact about literary periods, or grammatical information about
adjectival clauses. Both the step-by-step-to-competence model and the
body-of-knowledge model have been recognized for many years as inadequate
for English teaching. The 'traditional' English teaching we have characterized in the previous chapter was the product of an attempt to fuse the
two. This model has in turn proved inadequate. On the classroom side,
the wide range of ability to be taught in the comprehensive school, and

often in the same class, could not be handled in class lessons which were
based on it. It proved inadequate on the more academic side because its
account of language itself, of the nature of language learning, and of the
real value of literature were all found wanting by the scholars on whose
judgement the sanction for a school education ultimately rests. At the
same time, a large proportion of English teaching concerned itself with
the close study of literary works, and generations of teachers have done
inspired and inspiring work with often dreary materials handled in ped-
estrian ways. We shall explore some of the subsequent changes in English
teaching in our closing chapter. At this point it is necessary to answer the
question: what model would we suggest instead?

An alternative model

It is not an evasion to say first that to look for a model may be to ask the
wrong kind of question. If we are looking for a pattern of teaching, we are
possibly looking for something which can be done with whole classes,
where every pupil does the same thing at the same time. That kind of
model we cannot offer. Only a limited proportion of English work can be
done on such a basis. This is because even in a streamed class the variation
between pupils is enormous, in those respects which bear on English. A
class may have been very carefully streamed so that its pupils are within
only a point or two of having the same I.Q., or so that all its pupils can
comfortably master G.C.E. O-Level mathematics in four years. But however
homogeneous a class may be in any selection of educational respects, it
will present a staggering range of competence with language and an equally
wide range of personal and emotional maturity. It may not be the duty of
the English teacher to reduce this diversity, but it is clearly his obligation
to respond to it. The practices of traditional English teaching have usually
concealed this variation, not always to the advantage of the least successful
pupils in a class.

Carried to a logical conclusion this position would convert all English
teaching to a process of individual instruction for every pupil, which on
the face of it is wildly impractical. We shall explore in some detail, however,
the ways in which a fair compromise can be achieved. One element in our
model will be the systematic use of small groups. The central tasks of English
are to foster the personal growth of children and to increase their capacity
to use language for all those purposes which their lives make necessary. If
we had to give this view a catch-phrase label, we would call it a 'competence

and identity' model. We think it peculiarly important to see the two
components of this model, not as distinct and separate entities, but as
inter-penetrating elements: an adolescent whose competence with language
is supremely gifted may so lack a sense of his own identity or a sensitive
awareness of people as to be able to use his language skills only for destructive ends. In the same way, a child of 12 who is mature and sensitive beyond
his years will be unable to turn these virtues to any account if he is seriously
deficient in selecting what to say to people and how to say it.

By 'identity' in this context we mean rather more than the narrow
definition of the term in formal educational psychology. We mean, certainly,
the individual's understanding of himself as a person distinct from other
persons, and of the ways in which he resembles some and differs from
others. But we also have in mind a conception of identity in which the
emotional growth and awareness of the child is cushioned against the thousand natural shocks that childhood especially is heir to, so that the child
is enabled to explore the world of feelings and pains and pleasures in a
supportive environment. The English teacher is privileged here because
he is the purveyor (to put it no higher) of a range of literature which finds
no other point of entry into the school curriculum, and if he can select it
with insight and mediate it with skill he can make a permanent and
incomparable difference to the personal lives, to the identities, of his
pupils. We shall have much to say in later chapters about the competence
aspect of our model, but the identity aspect should come first because it
has proved for thousands of children the source of the motivation to 'learn
to use words', as T.S. Eliot put it. It will perhaps clarify the matter to give
two examples.

One of them comes from a primary school in a rural area of intense
cultural and linguistic impoverishment. The staff, uneasy about the slow
progress being made with workbooks and instruction about grammar and
parts of speech, worried even more by the children's reluctance to talk
than by their slowness at reading, discussed the problem at length. They
concluded that behind the poverty of language lay poverty of experience,
so they set out to build a curriculum to put this right. Some of the changes
were very ordinary. The paintings on the walls were changed every fort-
night. There was a film once a week. Some classes had doubled story-time.
The library van came sooner. The organized journeys happened more often
and went further. Some of the changes were less ordinary. The teachers
believed firmly that they should not try to take the children too fast or
into things too strange. So every child's personal hobby was supported and

expanded. The community was combed for other hobbies, and the grown-ups came in to demonstrate. A parent ran a tiny once-a-week bookstall, and brought in a pile of Sunday papers every Monday.

The teachers based their English teaching on the same principle of building on what the children already knew about. One class, mostly aged 9, was to 'do an assembly' about the flood. Looking for material, the teacher came across John Heath-Stubbs' poem 'The History of the Flood'. It is too long to quote here, but can be found in Copeman and Gibson's splendid anthology *As Large as Alone* (Macmillan). It begins with seven pairs of lines like this:

> Bang Bang Bang
> Said the nails in the Ark.
>
> It's getting rather dark
> Said the nails in the Ark.

Seven children, with triangles, chanted these lines to a stately banging. Most of the rest played the animals, but in mime instead of head-dresses (costume can easily obscure the real demands of drama). In the middle of the poem comes this:

> So Noah sent forth a Raven. The Raven said 'Kark!
> I will not go back to the Ark.'
> The Raven was footloose,
> He fed on the bodies of the rich—
> Rich with vitamins and goo.
> They had become bloated,
> And everywhere they floated.
> The Raven's heart was black,
> He did not come back.
> It was not a nice thing to do:
> Which is why the Raven is a token of wrath,
> And creaks like a rusty gate
> When he crosses your path; and Fate
> Will grant you no luck that day:
> The Raven is fey:
> You were meant to have a scare.
> Fortunately in England
> The Raven is rather rare.

The clear-voiced boy who read these lines showed a certain relish in 'vitamins and goo'. And a week or so later the teachers learned that the line 'That was not a nice thing to do' had become part of the children's playground conversation. Again, this received a matter-of-fact recognition of the familiar:

> Then the animals came ashore—
> There were more of them than before:
> There were two dogs and a litter of puppies;
> There were a tom-cat and two tib-cats
> And two litters of kittens—cats
> Do not obey regulations.

One of us was watching a class of boys and girls aged 13. The teacher was a strict but adventurous young English specialist who had asked for guidance about 'teaching poetry'—something he had not attempted very often. The children were fairly able, and had become unusually well-read for their age under the influence of the teacher. Rather diffidently, he distributed a duplicated sheet on which was the following:

> anyone lived in a pretty how town
> (with up so floating many bells down)
> spring summer autumn winter
> he sang his didn't he danced his did
>
> Women and men (both little and small)
> cared for anyone not at all
> they sowed their isn't they reaped their same
> sun moon stars rain.

The class made far more of this poem than merely its performance for assembly. The vignettes provided starting-points for art-work. There were stories about evil omens. There were investigations in folklore. There were two children who asked what a hierarchy was (the poem refers to 'insects in their hierarchies') and produced a diagram for the school, with the chairman of the managers at the top. Two boys felt sure the poet was wrong in classifying Galapagos tortoises among the reptiles, and started themselves off on a huge project about reptiles, which was to lead them to several zoos. But the object of the exercise had been to give children a chance to learn through experience, and all these instances of 'spin off' are incidental to this. The teacher remembers, as much closer to her aims, how seven children, each of them an only child from an isolated cottage or farmhouse, discovered for the first time in their lives how to keep exact time with six others on the triangle. The headmaster remembers the barely perceptible change in the boy who narrated the poem: he seemed to begin to learn, in some strange way, that his loud voice, taken in hand, might stop getting him into trouble and have its uses.

children guessed (but only a few
and down they forgot as up they grew
autumn winter spring summer)
that noone loved him more by more

when by now and tree by leaf
she laughed his joy she cried his grief
bird by snow and stir by still
anyone's any was all to her

someones married their everyones
laughed their cryings and did their dance
(sleep wake hope and then) they
said their nevers and slept their dream

stars rain sun moon
(and only the snow can begin to explain
how children are apt to forget to remember
with up so floating many bells down)

one day anyone died i guess
(and noone stooped to kiss his face)
busy folk buried them side by side
little by little and was by was

all by all and deep by deep
and more by more they dream their sleep
noone by anyone earth by april
wish by spirit and if by yes.

Women and men (both dong and ding)
summer autumn winter spring
reaped their sowing and went their came
sun moon stars rain

                                                            e e cummings

First the teacher read the poem through to the class, quietly, slowly, savouring its echoes. He looked round at the baffled faces. Is it true, he asked, that children are apt to forget to remember? A few nods about the room. And that down they forget as up they grow? Embarrassed silence. Taking another tack, he read the third stanza again and read on into the fourth, stopping abruptly on 'cried his grief'. After a pause, he jumped to 'laughed their crying', and repeated the two phrases, side by side. A tentative hand in the second row:
    Is noone a *person*, sir?
    If so, who's the other person?
Pause. Another pupil, one of the boys:
    Oh! I see: anyone's the bloke and noone's 'is wife!

Then who are someones and everyones? asked the teacher, and he read
the fifth stanza once more. 'Said their nevers'? What's he driving at?
Well . . . it's saying something you've promised you wouldn't, ever . . .
'And laughed their cryings'? Long pause.
Makin' fun of somethin' awful, like the yobbos does . . .
The teacher paused, knowing only too well that some incipient members of
that category were there in the room.
And 'slept their dream'?
Took 'em literal, never 'ad any ambition, like.
The talk was slow-moving, tentative, infinitely *delicate* in its exploration,
not merely of the text itself, but of its immediate, acutely felt implications
for the children themselves, and their daily lives. The teacher did not labour
the explication of every shred of the symbolism. He harked back to the play
they had read the previous term, Thornton Wilder's *Our Town* (Longman),
and the comparison with another way of dealing with death was
illuminating. After the thirty-five minutes of the lesson, with the bell nearly
due, he read the poem through again, tentatively and steadily.
Well? he said, looking round.
It's beautiful . . .—the sort of admission that children of 13 do not make
lightly.
That's all?
Yes OK, said a boy, all of a hurry, but it ain't soppy: it's got my two
uncles to a T!
One would rarely have the reward of observing such reverberating,
tense encounters in classrooms, but this lesson is not a mere anecdote. It is
an example of precisely what we meant by 'select with insight and mediate
with skill'. The boy who saw his uncle pinned down, defined, was being
enabled to bring his own experience of people into focus, and to make a
start on the long process of establishing his own identity in terms which
satisfied his intelligence as well as his feelings. Classroom experience of
this quality, repeated and elaborated over several years, affects people and
makes them, if only very slightly, different from what they would otherwise have become. And while a treatment of literature that relies for its
impact on 'great moments' of insight or experience is a foolish one, because
it assumes that all children are influenced in the same way by the same kind
of literary experience, such moments bring home to us that being an English
teacher can be profoundly rewarding.
    The poetry lesson just described is an example of a kind of teaching
which ought not to happen very often. It is strongly teacher-dominated,
and the use of a very puzzling poem could be regarded as intended,

consciously or otherwise, to strengthen this dominance, especially with an able class. This teacher needs to develop the use of small groups to explore the meanings of poems which are perhaps more readily penetrable by children of this age, and to explore them in a deliberately less directed fashion. The pupils concerned need to have learned, over a period of time, that such explorations may have many different outcomes: another poem, a short story, a painting, a multi-voiced reading on tape, a setting to music, or whatever the original may stimulate the group to produce.

The model in practice
If it is a business which cannot be adequately described as the transmission of a body of knowledge or the cumulative building of skills, how then may it be described? Our answer to this question has to be a practical one: it can only be described in terms of the activities in which pupils engage in the classroom. Because one element in our model is a competence with language, these activities are best viewed as language-using ones. All use of language is for the purpose of communication, and this in turn is a two-way process. The activities which use language, therefore, fall into pairs, each with a receptive and productive member. Talking hangs together with listening, and reading with writing. These four activities constitute the basis of classroom English. Talking is by far the most important of these, because it is the means of communication which will dominate the practical lives of the overwhelming majority of our pupils. The emphasis here is on talking, rather than the much more formal and difficult activities of speech-making or debate. The importance of talk hardly needs stressing, yet it is far from occupying its proper place in the curriculum: a majority of school pupils are given careful instruction in observing outdated conventions in writing letters, yet receive virtually no guidance on how and how not to conduct an intelligible telephone conversation. Talking and its corollary, listening, form the bedrock of our English curriculum.

The second series of activities to be built into English work is the range of activities associated with reading. We shall deal with this at greater length in Chapter 5. Here we would mention only two key points. The preoccupation with reading as a *skill* has led to an emphasis on schematic instruction which has far outrun the real need for it. There are very few reading schemes which really need all the 'extension readers' with which most of them are equipped. If a child is ready to move beyond the reading scheme into 'extension readers', he is in fact ready to move beyond books written with an eye chiefly on the simplicity of the language, to books written chiefly to tell a story to children of a particular age. Secondly, many teachers in the past have bemoaned the fact that some children 'do not read at home', and never do any 'outside reading'. If this is true, the response of the English teacher is simple and direct: supply the books that are needed, and bring the reading 'inside'.

We shall deal with writing as fully as space allows in Chapter 6, and with the problems of how to cope with its output in Chapter 7. Just as we want to see pupils who *are readers*, rather than children who *can read*, so we want to see young people who are writers rather than people who can write. The written form of expression, however, is one which many children of 9 and 10, and some older still, have not found easy. There is a lasting problem here, of how to balance the school's legitimate demand for written output, with the danger that asking the child to write too much for his current powers may inhibit him from writing at all. This is why there is an important place for other modes of expression than writing, especially for drama and mime. Delicate or painful situations and experiences can be acted out more easily by many children than they can be written about. The dramatized material in turn can stimulate and extend the writing. Educational drama is a controlled and sophisticated form of an activity which nearly all young children engage in. It has the additional virtue of being an alternative medium to writing, so that material can be switched from one medium to another without difficulty.

To view English as a set of activities—reading and writing, talking and listening—is not quite the same thing as viewing English as something which has identifiable or measurable 'results' in the form of written, spoken, or heard material. Nor is it necessary to see an English class as one in which one activity in particular is taking place. Another example illustrates this readily. A group of 12 year olds has been supplied with a tape-recorder (possibly the most useful single piece of equipment ever invented for English teachers) and given a brief to make a radio-play on the opening of a novel. They have chosen to do Charles Dickens' *Great Expectations*, partly because they have seen the extract from the opening of David Lean's film of the book, available from the British Film Institute. (See Sources and Resources 1, p.146.) The group of six or seven pupils has to start by listening to the chapter read aloud, working out in discussion how to translate its events and, much more difficult, its atmosphere, into sound. The difficulty lies in the fact that Dickens' imagery in this chapter is intensely visual. In reaching a solution to this difficulty the group will engage in a great deal of talk. This will be to some degree appreciative, focusing on the text and what the novelist was trying to achieve. But most of it will be transactional (see p.77), designed to seek solutions, try them out, develop suggestions, evaluate first attempts, decide what to put in and leave out, and so on. As things take shape, some of the outline of the radio version will have to be written down. When some of the material has been taped, it will be listened to with critical intensity, and modified and improved. The four basic activities of English are all involved, and trying to disentangle them is a fruitless exercise: they are all happening at once.

One other implication of this example, which is much nearer to the practice of most experienced English specialists than our previous example on p.22, is that good work in English can rarely, if ever, be completed within the compass of a single lesson. This adds to the difficulty not only of recording what is going on in traditional terms, but also of evaluating the work. We shall regularly refer to activities in English on the assumption that the best ones take much longer than a lesson or two. We shall also take it almost for granted that there may be a crucial difference between what seems to be happening on the surface and what is happening in reality. The group of children trying to make a model theatre may in reality be learning more about using spoken language to solve practical problems than about the design of theatres, though that too may enter into the matter. The child who sits silently through a group's sustained discussion of a story may be learning more about the role of listener than is immediately evident. Just as the fruits of English teaching are bound to be slow in emerging, so the realities of the English class may be very difficult to identify as well as to evaluate.

All this may suggest that English teaching is a rather formidable mystery: it would seem so much easier to reach for the nearest textbook or give a standard class lesson on the use of the question-mark. This is not really so. There is now a considerable store of experience and technique available, and it is our aim to compress and interpret this for the non-specialist, in as practical and helpful a way as possible. We would not attempt this if we did not believe that most teachers who have taught English in this way have found the process more rewarding and the results more enduring than what they did before. At this point we need only note the central objective, which is to create a workshop environment, in which children can easily engage in any of the basic activities of English, or any combination of these, as their own capacities and the skills of the teacher allow. The identity of the child is intimately related to his competence in using language to formulate that identity and organize his experience. The competence of the child in the use of language is developed only by using language, and the emphasis in this book will therefore be on what the pupil does and why he does it, not on 'what the teacher teaches'.

'What the teacher teaches' is put in quotation marks because without them the phrase would suggest a teacher-dominated classroom, and many English specialists would find it offensive. If there is to be a smooth continuity between work in the 9 to 13 age range and the later work of many English specialists, teachers of the former should appreciate how widespread is the belief that English has no place for the conventionally dominant teacher. Children will not succeed in English if they are not motivated to talk, listen, read, and write as individuals, and the development of self-directed work on self-selected topics and materials is of supreme importance in this. If there is no movement away from the tutelary direction of the teacher before the age of 13, pupils will go on to their upper-secondary schooling with a fixed set of attitudes that put the English teacher in a quite false position. If children of 13 believe their English teacher to be a sole authority (whether on spelling or style or literary taste), their own work as pupils will never gain any inner momentum and will lack commitment and conviction. The English work of the 9 to 13 range has to develop a capacity for self-determination in the pupil. Putting this policy into effect means refusing to tell children what to choose from the library, refusing to answer the questions which show excessive dependence (such as 'How much are we to write?'), and reinforcing on every possible occasion those instances where a pupil follows the spirit of his own strivings rather than the letter of the textbook's prescription. One part of the 'identity' side of our model, that is to say, obliges the teacher to see his pupils, and to relate to them, not so much as pupils but as people.

Language development

There is a much wider question, however, which calls for some kind of answer before we proceed to practicalities. This is the issue of language development. What can we say about the ways in which the language of 9 year olds changes during the ensuing four years? What really happens in the language development of this phase of life? An honest answer is that nobody knows, in the detailed, scholarly sense in which we 'know' what happens to the chemicals involved in a test-tube reaction. For to provide that kind of knowledge would require a larger research project than any yet provided for a linguistic inquiry. In the absence of such an investigation, we have to fall back on fragmentary and subjective approaches, which do little more than organize and perhaps clarify existing intuitions. (See, for example, C. and H. Rosen, *The Language of Primary School Children*, Penguin.) Alternatively, we can inspect the language demands made on children by their schools, and explore the kind of questions we ought to be asking, as we shall attempt to do here.

There are two ways of looking at a phenomenon like the language of children aged 9 to 13. One way is to treat it as development—that is, as the language aspect of general physical and intellectual growth. This approach is one reason that many educationalists refer to 'language development'. The fact of the matter is, however, that language is not innate, but learned. We speak quite properly of physical development, because the potential for growing to full size, height, and weight is innate. But we do not speak of the musical development of a child learning to play the piano. We should not let the common phrase 'language development' mislead us into supposing that language is not also, like playing the piano, something to be *learned*. The ways in which it is learned may very well be quite different, but that does not alter the principle.

Furthermore, the evidence of research into the brain and its development suggests that for most children those parts of it which control language are fully developed by the age of 9 if not somewhat earlier. So we should look at language changes after the age of 9 as the product of some process of learning. The difficulty of doing this by the before-and-after methods of normal educational research is formidable. Such research has to take a particular phenomenon which is finite, and measure it at two stages in time. Language is not finite. That is its peculiar nature: the elements which compose it—grammatical structures and vocabulary—may be finite, but the number of combinations of them which the ordinary native speaker can make is almost certainly infinite. This in turn may mean that language cannot validly be subjected to research by means of a sampling technique, and it will be many years before we know as much about language in children as we know, for instance, about mathematical perception.

What we can do is to study, not the learner and what he learns, but the language which he is normally assumed to have learned at particular stages. This requires the approach of the descriptive linguist. The age of 9 provides a useful starting point, because it corresponds to the reading age which is the official definition of literacy. We can usefully compare the skills expected of the average 9 year old with those expected of the average child of 13.

Perhaps the most striking difference between these two sets of skills is one which has little immediately to do with school at all. A child of 13 whose language behaviour, in a social or family setting, was that of a 9 year old would present something of a problem to most adults who had to have dealings with him. In particular, the kinds of conversation he could take part in, and the kind of part he could take, would be very much more limited than with a normal child of 13. This refers not only to what he says and how he says it, but to his readiness to listen to others, his ability to follow what they say and respond to it, and his ability to use language as a medium of social intercourse. The child of 13 normally persuades other children to do things with him in ways quite different from those used at the age of 9. He can usually use language to find things out for himself with much greater freedom and independence. He is, or should be, much more skilful at describing experience, realistically or imaginatively. These differences are so general and so marked that we are shocked not to find them. The 9 year old who talks like a much older child is an oddity, while the opposite phenomenon is cause for anxiety.

It is when we try to pin these general differences down to concrete detail that we find difficulty. It should in fact be possible to study and identify the ways in which the two age groups differ in the way they use, for example the rich resources of English for conveying meaning by intonation, but the study of intonation in spoken English is a very new and technical business. Problems also affect the study of children's language in social settings: the presence of a microphone and a tape-recorder will make a significant change in the language context. But enough has been said to make it clear that the social uses of language have to be learned just as the more academic uses do, and that the school may well have an important role in making this learning possible.

The school also faces children with a very different set of language-using situations from those encountered at home. One part of the normal child's language learning, then, will be that of mastering the many variations in his use of language which arise from its varying settings. This is at its most obvious in the matter of formality: children of 13 have usually learned, sometimes the hard way, that certain settings or relationships call for language used in a much more formal way than others, and many children learn to make adjustments accordingly without being conscious of doing so. This was very shrewdly perceived by a secondary headmaster who insisted on teaching every 13 year old class in his school twice a week on the grounds that the children needed to learn how to talk to headmasters without anxiety.

When we turn to written language, we can see this contrast between the language competence of 9 year olds and that attributed to 13 year olds by looking closely at the schoolbooks employed for them. The two groups of material differ quite sharply, in three main ways. First, secondary school books use many more of the orthographic resources of the writing-system: capital letters, italics, roman and arabic numerals, layout in note form, under-lining and other ways of conveying emphasis, deliberate variations in the widths of margins and the spaces between chapters or paragraphs. Secondly, the vocabulary and syntax of secondary materials are much wider and much more complex, particularly in the structure of the clauses and their order in the sentence. Third, there will be much more freedom in the secondary material in the length and weight of the units the sentences belong to. The links between them will be more subtle, too: for example, a fictional or historical narrative will use many different ways of identifying who is who in a narrative, what events occur in what time relationships, and how the cause and effects of events are inter-related.

In short, the learning that has to take place through written language and its interpretation (its 'reading', if you like) is prodigious. It is not any less a process of learning because few schools give lessons in it: the learning is best treated as built-in to the child's experience in other ways. Thus, the case for educational drama includes the argument that it helps children to learn the social uses of language more effectively than lessons on that topic would do. The case for project work includes the argument that it brings children to grips with a much wider variety of written language than they would meet in conventional classroom English. The case for a régime centred on children's literature read in whole books by the children themselves includes the argu-ment that only in this way will they experience written text as something which can both go on for a long time and be enjoyable. In all three instances the specifically linguistic learning that is taking place will be happening, as it should be happening, unobtrusively.

An example of this principle can be found in the punctuation of direct speech. Many primary schools try to teach children to do this as second-year juniors. Many secondary English teachers find themselves having to teach it all over again to every year in the school. The efficiency of the teaching would seem to be rather low in either case. From the linguistic point of view, the important thing is to start at the beginning, which is with the read-ing of conversations written *for* the pupils, not *by* them. To ask children to punctuate conversation without making sure they can interpret written dia-logue is really asking them to use an oar before they know what a boat is. And the learning can best take place by asking for the conversations to be read aloud or dramatized, with a minimum of explicit attention to the punctuation marks unless and until they make a difference to the speech. A class which has read a great many varied novels suited to its age and interests will acquire this mastery of speech marks almost without noticing it. When the time comes for them to use them, however, possibly by the age of 10 in the case of able children, the teacher has to convert this familiarity into a mastery of the formal rules. This will be impossible if the pupil's experience of written language has been confined to textbooks and comics, and even at best is difficult. In our observation most secondary textbooks treat these rules as content for two or three lessons, whereas they probably need much more time. Once learned, the punctuation will be quickly forgotten (as it often is) if the child's teachers, not only of English, fail to show that it matters.

Language skills are *skills*: that is, abilities whose continued use does not entail repeating the effort of learning them, but which atrophy if they are not used. The 'development fallacy' about language may lead us to suppose that many aspects of language which are in fact learned ought somehow to be retained as if they were the product of growth. But there is very little in the language learning of children above the age of 9 which they can be expected to retain simply as part of the order of nature.

What has been said about language learning does more than suggest that 'language development' is an unfortunate phrase. It implies that a reading-age score is only a very partial measure of a child's state of learning. Indeed, most specialist English teachers in junior schools deplore the tendency to regard a reading age as a meaningful indication of a child's progress in English. Reading ages reflect a very narrow test of a very narrow group of skills. However, they do reflect something real in the children they refer to, whereas the idea that a *book* can have a reading age is the sheerest nonsense. Publishers often indicate the age of child for which some books seem suitable but these gradings are general, intuitive, and often belied in practice.

Chapter 3

Organizing the English class

Timetabling

We may accept that English as a subject is a unity which is not well served by being divided into components, but there may be practical difficulties in the way. Normal middle and secondary school timetables envisage an allocation of one fifth or one sixth of the week for English, and often less. In a timetable divided into forty-minute periods English will usually receive six single, or three double periods. Apart from the temptation to treat these sessions as separate units, the non-specialist often finds himself sharing a class's English work, taking perhaps two of the sessions only. A few teachers have the freedom or the duty to treat English as something wholly integrated with other elements in the curriculum. This chapter tries to suggest an approach to English which can be applied in either situation.

If there is any choice in the matter of timetabling, the non-specialist teacher new to English would be wise to ask for a double period and the balance in singles, with the double one ideally at the end of an afternoon. He would also do well to take all the English with one class rather than a snippet with each of several classes. The merit of the double period lies in its scope for developing new ways of working, especially those which take time both to get going and to clear up at the end. It allows the teacher to show substantial pieces of film, to arrange for an outside speaker, or to take the class on a visit with less disruption of the timetable. Most experienced English teachers prefer the larger unit, and some would ask for all their time to be in double period sessions. Organizing work over such blocs of time calls for experience, however, and one a week is enough to start with. Even so, it can provide a focus for the week's work, and the inexperienced non-specialist can always divide other double periods up into two singles.

We shall write this and the following chapters on the working assumption that many teachers have to work to a timetable of some sort. This does not imply that we in any way disapprove of the integrated day[1], so long as English

does not get lost in the integration, and teachers who practise it will find that
the approach we suggest can be adopted more readily in their flexible settings than otherwise. Nor does our assumption imply that we approve of
rigid timetabling in the junior school; on the contrary, when it is imposed
on a teacher who is trained and inclined to do without it, the imposition
may hinder valuable work.

We shall also assume that the reader is responsible for all the English
work of a class. Where this is not the case, we would suggest that the two
teachers concerned should avoid a simple division of work like 'You do
the poetry and I'll do the rest' or 'You've got them in the hall that period,
so you do the drama.' The real need is for more frequent consultation,
leading to much closer linking up and some exchanging of activities between
the two teachers, and leading both of them to approach their agreed parts
of the work along broadly similar lines or at least in ways which differ
acceptably. Children should not be expected to cope with conflicting
instructions from two teachers of the same key subject.

Arranging the classroom

The use and arrangement of the furniture in a classroom are basic. Again,
there may be practical problems, not least with the schoolkeeper or
cleaners, but something can usually be done to improve the most unpromis-
ing of classrooms. The aim should be to achieve an arrangement which fits
the activities going on within it: children should not be expected to watch a
video-tape for forty-five minutes sitting on the edge of a table because it
seemed too much trouble to re-arrange the chairs properly. It was implicit
in the last chapter's account of the modern English curriculum that the
essential need of the English class is *space*, and, in particular, spaces which
can be adjusted quickly. If children are to be free to undertake improvisation, group talk, group reading, or making a tape, or whatever else is called
for, they need a classroom fitted with chairs and tables that are easily moved
and stacked. (The Pel Forme range is a good example.) But even traditional
desks can be grouped together so that fours and sixes of children can sit at
them and form groups. The details of these arrangements need thinking out,
so as to provide as large an area of free space as possible, for drama work, for
sitting together for story-time, and much else.

Removing the teacher's desk from its dominant position also gives the
teacher a stronger, not a weaker, disciplinary position. It removes the confron-
tation between teacher and class, and changes the nature of the teacher's control to a management of individuals and groups rather than of a whole class.

Once the teacher and class have adjusted to a group-based classroom (if adjustment is necessary), the relationships which can develop are potentially much more open. In the flexible classroom, too, the teacher has the freedom to re-focus his pupils' attention on a new activity by requiring them to re-arrange the furniture. The main constraint on this flexibility is the need for a classroom area loaded with basic materials, which should not be confused with the teacher's stock-cupboard, and will often be next to or part of the teacher's desk. Pupils of 9 and upwards should be trained to obtain basic materials from this source for themselves, since the teacher is not making good use of his professional time by acting simply as a stock-dispenser. (His control over consumption lies in the work he plans for the class.) In fact the teacher will not spend a great deal of time at his desk. For reasons which we elaborate on later, discussion with pupils about their work belongs in the pupils' groups, with the teacher moving about among them as guide, problem-solver, and asker of challenging questions. The teacher has done his part of the work beforehand: in the classroom he is engaged with the pupils while they do their part.

We shall be laying emphasis on the role of classroom talk, and such talk is one of the main reasons for advocating group organization. Even in a school where all desks have to remain in rows, however, through some dog-matic rule, pupils can be encouraged to work in pairs to resolve simple questions, as a first step to genuine discussion. Once pupils who are quite unused to interacting with one another in class have become accustomed to this kind of pair-talking, it is easy to move a step beyond this. Some of the pairs can be asked to turn round and face the pair behind them to constitute groups of four. The important thing is to avoid being imprisoned by the surface appearance of the classroom. If the desks need to be moved about, and replaced afterwards, it is wise to take a little time establishing a routine, under which children can and do become very skilled at transforming a formal classroom astonishingly quickly and quietly.

There are many ways of making a classroom a pleasant place to work in, and the teacher who does not have to move about among several rooms is at an obvious advantage in using display for this purpose, but even the teacher who uses a colleague's room only occasionally can seek the latter's agreement to the decoration of his room for a clear educational purpose. This does not mean we have to try to cover every inch of wall space (let alone windows), but display is valuable as an incentive for pupils' written work, and screens or stands designed for this purpose are common in many schools.

Planning one's time

After his pupils are disposed in groups, how is the teacher to organize his
time with them? It is very desirable to think in terms of substantial spans
of time rather than of sequences of individual lessons. Children who are
engaged in one central activity are in much less need of a sedulous linking-
up of each individual lesson to its predecessor. We would go so far as to
commend the use of the time scale of half a term, settling on a broad plan
for it and elaborating the details within those naturally defined starting
and finishing points. For any large block of time it is necessary to have an
integrating or guiding idea, and in recent years the great majority of specialist teachers of mixed-ability classes in this age range have come to use a
thematic approach. With older children it is feasible to plan work in terms
of a sequence of literary works, but children under 13 do not readily see
the abstract ideas which give such sequences their unity. With under 13
year olds it is wiser, if one is using a literature-based approach, to take a
single work and to build the month's or the half-term's work round it. Such
a plan provides enough time to take a work of some substance and still allow
for the class to listen to the teacher reading large parts of it aloud. We have
seen outstanding examples, by non-specialist teachers, using books most of
which are listed in Sources and Resources II (see p.153). One example used
H.M. Morrow's *The Splendid Journey* (Heinemann) in a way which turned
the work into a half-term project on the American west and exploited to
the full, and quite properly, the teacher's expertise as a geographer. Another
class aged 13 did the same, guided by a historian, and included in its work a
reading, by a group of seven boys, of almost every available book about the
early west from the report of the official inquiry into the Custer disaster
down to John Steinbeck's *Grapes of Wrath* (Penguin). Short stories and films
can act in a similar way as the initial stimulus to a sustained, thematic piece
of work.

Using a particular book as the base for a block of work is infinitely more
than 'doing a reader', although it usually requires every pupil to have a copy.
To take an example used with a class aged 9, based on Edith Unnerstad's
Saucepan Journey (Puffin): the teacher read the first three chapters aloud
before distributing copies, and sensed her pupils' puzzlement over the
Swedish names. Two sessions were devoted to Sweden, its places and persons
and their names: the Swedish Embassy supplied an out-of-date copy of the
Stockholm telephone directory, and there were workcards for groups to
follow, using this, an Esso road map, the only geography textbook available,
and the usual reference books. Meanwhile a group was preparing to dramatize
the hectic, overcrowded domestic life of the family, and their version included

a scene with a visitor, invented by the group, who had to be told all the information given in the book by the narrator. The class did a written story about the parents' early life together, and two boys tried to make a weight for a pressure-cooker which would whistle like the invention in the book. The girls who were in the horsey phase revelled in the assembling of the caravans and horses, and models were made of the whole outfit. The work went on through the book, roughly at the rate of two chapters a week, and the whole class turned the family's arrival in a strange village to sell their saucepans into a play for assembly. The teacher was able to find a Swedish visitor, who was entranced by the detail and depth of the questions asked as she went round from group to group. In answer to a request, she had to go away and write a Swedish version of an extract from the book (not having access to the original). It was put on the wall, and a cassette recording was made by the visitor for the children to listen to while they tried to decipher the text. At the end, some of the class had discovered the same author's two books for younger children, written about younger members of the same family (*The Urchin* and *Little O*, both Puffin), and these had to be read too. Additional stories about other members of the family were written as follow-up work; an interview, in which Little O was asked about the journey, was taped for radio; a map of the journey was made , with pictures and posters and signs to mark the events of the main book. This teacher had done French as a main subject at college, but her English teaching was inventive and exciting.

The natural alternative to taking a book and working outwards is to select a desired outcome and plan the work towards it—a class newspaper, or a tape-recorded documentary, for example. The 'radio ballads' and B.B.C. documentaries and 'Scrapbook' programmes offer many good models. Or one may take a story, have it turned into a play for actors or puppets, and aim at a production (a plan which could be used with some O-Level set books with advantage). A less gifted class can be started half-way along this kind of project by using a play script such as the Puffin edition of *St. George and the Dragon* and *Punch and Judy* edited by Diana John.

Either of these approaches will give coherence to the diverse elements of English, but the emphasis will vary with the stimulus or the outcome selected. Producing a taped documentary will lead to more talk than writing, while working from a book will probably lead to more reading and writing, and the good teacher will ring the changes in the light of the need to cater for each element adequately during a year. Because each group of pupils may work in distinctive ways, doing mainly writing at one time and mainly talking at another, the teacher's record-keeping needs to cover the work and its nature rather than assessments of results: notes are better than marks. What the notes might be about is discussed in Chapter 7.

The younger the class, the more important it becomes to have observable outcomes at an early stage. The same applies to older classes of less able pupils. The framework based on half a term may still apply, but the plan should provide children the satisfaction of seeing completed stages of the work at shorter intervals. The natural basis for these shorter segments is of course the school week, each one dealing with a new aspect of the underlying theme.

Thematic work—an example

Turning to a detailed, practical example of a sequence of lessons, we shall take a commonplace topic, 'Animals'. With half a term's work in mind, the teacher wants to concentrate on the pupils' development of writing and reading skills, and on the ability to write in more than one way for more than one end—for imaginative, functional, narrative, and poetic purposes. He wants also to encourage some conscious attention to the differences in one's writing which arise from changes in the audience it is intended for. Naturally he will succeed in this large aim more with some pupils than with others, but if he is to succeed at all *he must know what his general aims are*. It does not follow that his pupils will also know; their idea of the teacher's aim will be more concrete, such as producing a file or folder of work containing a variety of their own writing, pictures, photographs (often with writing about them), pieces of prose and poems from anthologies. Some groups may be asked to make selections of their work for display, which entails making evaluative judgements, and probably rewriting and correcting for the public situation of display.

Let us suppose that the teacher introduces his theme at the first convenient double session. The particular method will reflect local circumstances. As we write, a newspaper story tells of a boy badly mauled by a circus tiger he was training, which could lead to discussion of tame, half-wild, and wholly wild animals. This largely teacher-directed opening session might include slides of animals in zoos and in nature, taped or duplicated pieces of writing which illuminate the theme further—the 'tamed and shabby tigers' from Ralph Hodgson's 'The Bells of Heaven', William Blake's 'Tyger' (both in A.F. Scott's *Poems for Pleasure*, Book I, C.U.P.), and others spring to mind. Other starting points include a visit to a zoo or wild-life park, or a visit from someone with a collection of unusual pets. Here the experience often lies in the sense of touch, but sound, smell, and the sense of scale that pictures can never provide are all part of the value of having the real thing in the classroom. Another way into such a theme is to make or have made a set of pictures of fabulous beasts, pin them up round the room, and, with younger pupils especially, supply story-openings and useful sets of words. Working in groups or individually, the children work up stories of their own round the fabulous beasts, act them out, tell them aloud, or put them on tape. Teachers who work together in a junior school often develop well-prepared thematic projects for one class, and, rather than see the preparation wasted, exchange classes with a colleague.

There is no need to seek for the overtly spectacular in starting a project: latching on to items of current news is within every teacher's scope. There is a need for a certain opportunism, however, since classes vary a great deal in what they will respond to, but in general the carefully prepared opening is the key to a successful project. The best prepared opening may fall flat, however, and it is always wise to have a number of alternative lines to pursue, or indeed an alternative project altogether. But an opening session is an exploration between teacher and children: the talk should be allowed to run, the possibilities should be explored, as the children see them. If the opening is a visit, the attention of the children needs to be steered. Children need help in knowing what to look for, lest they come away with a confused jumble of impressions. Duplicated quiz sheets are like traditional poems in anthologies: hackneyed for the best possible reason, that they work well. (There are useful commercial examples, such as the *I Spy* series (Dickens Press) or Shire Publications' *Discovery* series, but they are better as examples to the teacher than used by the children themselves.) Somewhere early in a project on animals the children's experience of them should be tapped. Group talk can be a base for writing or drama or tape-recording about pets they have had or wanted, or other encounters with animals.

Developing the theme

By now we will be into the second or third session. It is time for the teacher to bring in a new stimulus, such as a literary one—a reading from Philippa Pearce's *A Dog so Small* (Puffin), which some children adore and others, perhaps understandably, detest, or Gerald Durrell's *My Family and Other Animals* (Penguin). Either of these will point to a worksheet to be issued to the pupils. The crucial step in a project with mixed-ability classes is the move away from work which involves the whole class to work in groups or as individuals. We give overleaf a sample worksheet: a duplicated list of group and individual assignments providing plenty of choice. It needs to be tailor-made and related to the materials available, and our example is deliberately somewhat of an ideal.

ANIMALS AND THE LANDSCAPE

You should aim to carry out at least six of these tasks. Choose them so that you cover a variety of work - descriptive writing, reading and copying poems, writing free verse, reading stories. If in doubt, see me.

1. Choose an animal that has its natural habitat in this country, and (i) write a brief description which could go into a book on natural history; (ii) write a free verse poem which tries to show something of the way the animal moves; (iii) write a story about it, bringing out the countryside it lives and moves in.

2. Spend some time watching closely an animal you know well Then write down everything you can find to say about its looks and behaviour for someone who will never see it.

3. Look in the project library for information about camouflage. Then read Turner's poem 'India' (copies from me) and write a poem of your own about a British animal that fits into its background.

4. Find out about greyhounds and coursing, noting the differences from fox-hunting. Write a short information sheet about these sports.

5. Write about a man hunting a fox <u>and</u> a fox hunting a rabbit. Describe them so as to bring out the similarities and differences.

6. Suppose you are a huntsman. Write a letter to the local paper in which a neighbour attacks fox-hunting; then write the short article in which you reply. Remember that the letter-writer is a <u>neighbour</u>.

7. Read one of the following and write a brief account of it, explaining what it is about and your opinion of it:

> John Masefield - 'Reynard the Fox'
> Henry Williamson - Tarka the Otter
> Ted Hughes - 'Esther's Tomcat'
> Philippa Pearce - A Dog so Small
> Richard Adams - Watership Down

8. Make a collection of poems about animals and the places they live in. Copy out four or five of them and add at least three more poems of your own.

9. Find out as much as you can about the coypu, and write an information sheet which explains how and why it has become a pest.

10. Fabulous animals: find out about the Yeti, the Minotaur, the Unicorn, and the Phoenix, with any other animals of legend and fable you can discover. Write a brief description of each and how they were supposed to live.

11. Write a free verse poem which tries to pin down exactly how a snake moves through the grass or a fish through water.

12. Read animal poems by D.H. Lawrence, John Clare, William Blake, Edward Thomas, and Ted Hughes. Copy out half a dozen poems by some of these authors and write some others of your own of a similar kind to go with them.

Work in pairs, in groups, or on your own, as you prefer. Present your work so that at the end you have assembled your own Book of Animals, with illustrations (drawings, photographs, etc.), by half-term. At least one of your tasks should be suitable for putting on the classroom wall display.

Of course, such a worksheet sets up a situation calling for a battery of materials and resources in the classroom. This is much less formidable than it sounds, and Sources and Resources I (pp.139 ff.) gives advice about where to go for it and how to go about it. But assembling the necessary materials *must* be done before the project starts. Once the materials have been assembled and the worksheet prepared (and the one will inevitably be influenced by the other), the sessions generate their own impetus, and the teacher is free to deal with the hundred and one questions and requirements the pupils will present. For the particular example we have given, the number of items on the sheet could be much longer, according to the resources available. In this instance, the teacher should assemble a combination of some of the following:

Wall-charts (e.g. those of the World Wild.Life Trust).

Classroom library (on block loan from school or public
   library service, which is usually available to private as well as maintained schools) containing fiction related to the theme and plenty of
   simple picture reference books.

Poetry anthologies in sets of three and four copies.
   (Several are devoted especially to animals, and can be found in the
   catalogues of O.U.P., Heinemann, and Penguin.)

A duplicated anthology of about 20 short poems selected with
   the age and ability of the class in mind.

Recordings, on tape or disc, of wild-life sounds and of
   stories. (This is the kind of material that Teachers Centres exist to
   make available.)

Slides, film-strips, and film-loops, for individual and
   group viewing. (Nuffield Science film-loops are useful here.)

Reproductions of appropriate paintings, as slides or for display.

A duplicated reference list of addresses to which *children* can write for
   information. (Note the caution on this point in Sources and
   Resources I, p.142.)

A stock of colour magazine supplements as a source of pictorial material
   for children to cut up and use for display.

In addition the teacher should arrange corporate experiences to be fed in when the impetus of personal or group study begins to wane. This may range from a serial reading of a book like Jack London's *White Fang* (Heinemann) to showing a film about insects (see the Petroleum Film Bureau catalogue for an example).

The precise number and nature of the tasks set out on a worksheet can be adjusted both to the abilities of the class and to the length of time available for the theme. It is also possible to select work-tasks in such a way as to create a particular emphasis in the language skills which are being strengthened, or to ensure coverage of all four aspects of language learning. But the worksheet should be viewed not as a prescription of pupils' work but as a base or starting point: children should be encouraged to develop their own, individual lines of inquiry.

Thematic work is not an orthodoxy which can be adopted as a substitute for previous approaches. Two helpful books about it are Geoffrey Summerfield's *Topics in English* (Batsford) and Alan Lynskey's *Children and Themes* (O.U.P).Some themes which have been used successfully with children between 9 and 13 include: The Seasons, The Four Elements, The Five Senses, Communications, The Supernatural, Christmas, Circuses, Fairs and Markets, Games and Pastimes, Night and Day, The Sea, Town and Country, Gypsies and Pedlars, Sun and Wind. The titles remain simple, and their elaboration will depend on the age group involved. A class of 10 year olds working on Communications is likely to make models and plays and writings about space-travel, but a class aged 12 may explore Clive King's *The Twenty-Two Letters* (Puffin) and more formidable books on the origin of writing, and a class older still may make some studies of communication between people who find it hard to make human contact. The last could well include Ruth Underhill's *Antelope Singer*. (Helen Morris's *Where's That Poem?* (Blackwell) is a useful source book for other poems and stories.) Communication, or the lack of it, between the generations is a theme of many novels and poems, too, but this is a mature topic for 13. Thematic work should incorporate some element of literature, if it is not firmly based on it, but a particular work may, as it were, 'take charge' of the theme. This has happened more than once with J. Meade Falkner's *Moonfleet* (Edward Arnold) and a theme about Smuggling. What starts out as a general theme can quite properly become a piece of topic work based on a single book, with the work widening out, in the case of *Moonfleet* for example, into studies of the period, its costume, coastal life, policing, excise system, and so on.

Mixed—ability teaching and the slow reader

With most middle school classes it is probably best to attach less weight to chronological age and to recognize the widely differing population within a class. The sexes mature very differently in this period, for one thing, quite

apart from differences of ability, which it is not in the children's interests to
accentuate overtly. But the natural anxiety felt about giving able children
enough to keep them engaged is more readily met by making quiet suggestions
to individual pupils, within the wider mixed-ability context—the extra book to
read, the more taxing writing task, the special investigation (like that given to
the gifted boy who found out exactly what sort of caravan could be made out
of the drays of a Swedish brewery). The same approach of keeping the excep-
tional pupil in the general group applies even more forcibly to the less able
pupil, whose performance is only made worse by too public a labelling of his
backwardness. If there are several such pupils, a strong visual/aural emphasis
to the work is called for, but if one has the problem of a number of non-
readers at the age of 9 or 10 it is desirable to seek advice, and to cast as much
as possible of their work towards language. All too often the non-reader at
9 has been a non-talker at 7, and is likely to be still inarticulate. Hence,
word-games of every kind should be added to the pattern, especially those
which make the pupil talk and read out loud the words being played with.
Beyond this, the participation of the less able in class activities can be eased
in several ways:

1.   *Grouping* should as a rule put a diversity of abilities in each group.
Most classroom groups are self-chosen, friendship based, and single sexed.
The teacher does not have to choose between this and ability-grouping. He
can set the class into self-chosen pairs and re-arrange the groups by varying
his combinations of pairs. He can also go much further, of course, making
a sociogram of the class and constructing the groups accordingly, or using
its information to help him place the isolated or rejected members of the
class. (For further guidance, which is essential before making this kind of
study, see K.M. Evans, *Sociometrics*, Routledge.) If the grouping can be
manipulated to put poorer readers and better readers together, with more
than one of each in a group, the former gain from the latter and the able
ones challenge each other.

2.   *Workcards* are an alternative to work-sheets, taking longer to prepare
but giving much more control over what goes on and directing the work of
the least able more firmly. Library catalogue cards are used for writing out
short, specific assignments, and the younger or less able child is not embarrassed by having to make choices. The cards can be colour-coded for level
of difficulty, and more than one copy may be needed, but they can help the
teacher to control the work of particular pupils closely (they can be very
useful with the trouble-maker, for example), by selecting a particular sequence of cards. But learning how to make rational choices and plan one's

work are essentials of schooling, and most children of 13 should be making such decisions for themselves. There is a good example of workcard technique in Macmillan's *Discovery Project* series, where each unit also contains reference books, a poetry anthology, and other resources designed for middle schools. As models, these cards are valuable, but they are made for a mass market, and the stamp of the teacher's individual mind and hand on a class's workcards seems to have a striking effect on the pupils' response.

3.   *Audio-visual aids* have been mentioned as useful with the less able, and it is now possible to put a teacher's instructions into aural as well as written form by using the Synchrofax machine (E.J. Arnold Ltd.). Essentially a tape-recorder, it plays up to four minutes of sound which is recorded on the underside of a stout, A4-sized, cardboard sheet, while the upper side shows related instructions in written form. This allows one to make what are in effect talking workcards which help with reading difficulties and enable the listeners to hear the speech over headphones. The Synchrofax sheets are easily stored and can be built up into a full stock. A sound-only method involves the use of cassette recording, and there are now many cassette players which children of 8 can operate easily. This method is not as valuable with non-readers as it is with the able, who can be set listening tasks of a high order of difficulty. The effect of these diverse methods of communication on children of varied abilities is much more important than it may seem, especially in motivating writing by the able as well as the less able.[3]

Conclusion

These approaches to organizing English may seem daunting at first sight, but they are in sum no more demanding of time than the mathematics work of the modern junior school class, although the apparatus is less easily purchased. The careful advance preparation it calls for does set the teacher free for his prime function in the classroom. Obviously the teacher must keep track of the work which each pupil appears to be engaged in—the work-assignment he is pursuing, or whatever it may be. But many teachers devise ways of getting children to make records of their work as an integral part of doing it, thus leaving the teacher freer for something he cannot delegate, something which is vital. No-one else can move about among the children as an adult speaker of English with whom the children can talk without a forced deference. No-one else, for most children, can help them, for many of them need help that will not damage the relationship between adult and child, and the teacher is in nothing more professional than in building and preserving that set of relationships. The teacher circulates about the room,

asking questions, probing ideas, nudging and pushing and kidding his
pupils through their experience of words, above all using language with
them—his language, without talking down and without the special tones
of voice that many adults reserve for talking to children. He moves about
unpredictably, using the vast incentive of his praise and the lesser (but
potent) force of his disapproval: getting the non-talkers to talk, challenging the glib to be explicit, taking each child at his or her own level, interacting with his pupils as a mature user of language. This is the one, irreplace-
able role of the teacher.

We have made no bones about English and its demands on the teacher,
for we are writing for the teacher who wants to do justice to English,
as well as for the probationer or the student. But a tentative experiment
for one block of time or with one class, well prepared, or as one might now
say well resourced, using the information given in Sources and Resources I,
will probably show that this approach is in the long run less demanding
rather than more. Teachers who have accepted this approach, and thrown
off the tyranny of the single lesson, have been taken by surprise at the
speed with which a stock of materials and resources can accumulate But it
is not in the end with the teacher and his burdens that justification lies: it is
with the pupil, and his motivation to extend, often unawares, the range
and depth of his command of English.

Chapter 4

Talking, listening, and drama

The last chapter was concerned with the part played by the teacher as an organizer and manager of learning situations. This chapter and the next two focus on the parts played by the pupil, taking in turn the central activities of English—talking, listening, reading, and writing.

Talking and listening

'Oral English' often appeared in the English programme of the past, but it was usually of a rather formal kind, such as debate or lecturettes. This reflected the more formal tradition of classroom situations, and, in part, a widespread belief that these particular speech situations were of some special importance. In the formal classroom, with the desks in rows and the focus of attention on the front of the room, it is normally required that only one person speak at once. Anyone who speaks is apt to be forced, albeit briefly, into the role of speaker addressing an audience. This is a legitimate exercise for some pupils, but it is not the only kind of speech situation, or indeed the kind which matters most in the 9 to 13 age range. There are many other kinds of talk, and it would be hard to exaggerate the role of the tape-recorder in opening the eyes and ears of educationists to the nature of the variety of talk. It has become possible to study closely examples of speech in many situations, and we now understand some of its grammatical and social features much more clearly than in the past. (See, for example, the account of Labov's work in P.S. Doughty *et al*, *Exploring Language*, Edward Arnold, pp.168—70.) We have learned that speech operates by regular patterns or rules just as written language does, but those of speech are much more complex than had been thought and quite different from those of written language. We know, too, that speech is of prime importance in language growth and development for all levels of age and ability. The effect of the invention of tape-recording on this understanding of language

is as revolutionary as that of the cine-camera was for the study of movement.
The teacher needs to share some of this new knowledge, which is fortunately
readily accessible (see Andrew Wilkinson, *The Foundations of Language*,
O.U.P.).

Our pupils speak a great deal more than they write in any normal situation,
with the possible exception of the classroom. Throughout our lives we all communicate linguistically with others, mainly by talking. We use talk to establish
our roles in relation to others, to engage with them socially, to get things done
and for all the other purposes for which we use language. The proportion of
communication that we do in writing is minor, but this does not mean that it
is not important whether one can do it. It does mean, however, that the traditional classroom's neglect of the diverse use of talk is open to criticism.

Talk as a productive skill has its receptive counterpart in listening. Pupils
gain much practice in listening to their teachers, but rarely do they get adequate practice in listening to each other or to strangers, and teachers have to
force themselves into listening adequately to what their pupils have to say.
(See Douglas Barnes in *Language, the Learner, and the School,* Penguin.) This
matter has been subject to extensive study in recent years, both as formal
research and as a part of teacher-training. Even where the teacher's main aim
is to elicit a spoken response from pupils (as in a 'discussion' lesson), teacher-
controlled situations *normally* show the teacher doing about 70% of the talking
This proportion seems to hold good whatever the size of the group and
throughout the secondary and undergraduate levels. Studies of classroom
language have also revealed that when teachers ask questions to which they
already know the answers, pupils try to guess what the teacher has in mind
rather than work out the solution to the problem posed. John Holt in
How Children Fail (Penguin) suggests that the latter activity is one of the
main sources of under-achievement in school.

An approach which meets the problem of the disproportion of speech and
writing in schools must create classroom situations where questions are more
open-ended, where ideas and queries originate from the pupil as well as from
the teacher, where talk in small groups can be the normal social situation for
exploring problems. As we have stressed, the arrangement of the classroom and
the planning of work are of crucial importance. The teacher needs actively to
plan himself out of the traditional role, so that he is free to circulate amongst
groups of children, listening to the talk and participating in it—not with authority derived from his status, but with authority derived from his being the
one mature and fluent user of language in the room.

The talk that the pupil engages in, however, needs to be purposeful. First,
though, there is a place for gossip and small-talk. A class engaging in group

work must at some stage form its groups, and time must therefore be allowed for the social relationships within each group to develop. In this phase of a group's life, gossip is important, whether the group is 9 or 19 years of age. But an established group faced with a problem or task will quickly move from gossip to relevant anecdote and on to generalization or comment which helps the group to new insight and new solutions. Such group talk is cyclic in nature: it does not move steadily from point to point, but moves rather in waves. A good example of this variation can be found in Part Two of *Language, the Learner, and the School*, where James Britton makes an extended analysis of a transcript of some girls discussing a short story. Britton's introductory comment sets the tone for much of the thinking about the role of spoken language that we are here endorsing:

> We want children, as a result of our teaching, to *understand*; to be wise as well as well informed, able to solve fresh problems rather than have learnt the answers to old ones; indeed, not only able to answer questions but also able to ask them.

If the teacher keeps the final outcome in mind, he need not worry if the route by which the children's talk reaches it is circuitous: talking round a problem is a first step to solving it for adults and children alike. If we want children to produce interesting writing, let them talk out its material together. In much the same way, our own work in teaching students and in in-service training has been an essential part of the process of writing this book, and each section of it has begun in a spoken context. It seems particularly odd therefore that children are so frequently expected to write without this prior preparation of talk.

Achieving this climate of group talk in the classroom requires that the children work in small groups, which can range from four to seven in number. The less experience the children have of group talk, the shorter the periods of time given to it have to be, and the more specific will be the task given each time. Much of the work will be done without the teacher's presence, since the teacher can be with only one group at a time. This can be an advantage, for the teacher needs to learn when to stand back and let a group get on with it. With several groups at work in the same room, of course, there will be a great deal of talk going on, and pupils need training and practice if they are to participate without interfering with the work of other groups. This in turn is an important reason for aiming at some kind of common practice in an English department in a secondary or middle school. Although group activity is normal enough in most junior schools, it is not often devoted to this most potent of all skills. For English, moreover, group talk should be as normal and natural a feature as field-work in geography or demonstrations in science, so that pupils come to expect it; and if they ask why they do it, they should be told.

Here is a typical introduction to a set of instructions issued to a class engaged on a project on 'Childhood'. The pupils were not very experienced in group work, and needed reassurance about the role they were to play as participants in groups.

Working in your groups, carry out as many as you can of the assign-ments listed below. You may always talk with each other in class about the work you are doing, but try to do it in such a way as not to disturb the other groups. It is best if you discuss each item you are working on as a group before writing about it.

Reading is essential to this project. Each member of the class should have read at least two books on the theme before the project ends. You can exchange your books, or read, in any lesson. When you find a book that you especially enjoy, don't forget to recommend it to others in your group.

Sources. You will find material to use in the project from personal experience (your own and other people's), literature, local research, material from libraries, newspapers, and magazines.

At the end of the project each group should have completed a folder which contains the results of what it has been doing. The group should itself select the work to be included to make up the final folder. Not everyone in the group needs to have been working on the same things of course. This will mean discussion and planning your programme of work together. At the end each folder will contain stories, essays, poems, facts and information, writing about books, and will be illustrated with drawings and pictures.

Even the worst designed classroom with the most old-fashioned furniture can be adapted to this work. Whatever the arguments with the school keeper, the desks must be arranged in groups so that the group can sit looking at one another and talking amongst themselves without distracting others. The teacher must be ready for, and encourage, a wide variety of activities going on at the same time, not all of it necessarily within the classroom. For example, pupils may be in animated conversation about a picture for the cover of the folder, while others are putting together a collage poster to advertise their folder (and engaging in much problem-solving talk meanwhile); another group may be elsewhere with a tape-recorder,

while yet others are moving from group to group administering a questionnaire
or gathering copy for a class newspaper. This multiplicity may look chaotic to
teachers unfamiliar with the integrated day of the junior school, but what
counts is the amount of real talk and real listening going on. All the tasks and
activities will be purposive, bearing on the end product chosen by the groups:
none of them is an 'exercise' *with no purpose beyond itself*. The key to this
purposiveness is a clear understanding of what the group is expected to achieve,
and this will be greatly helped if the group has taken part in formulating its
own goals. But the pace of talk cannot easily be forced, and the new group
will need time and patience before it gets down to fruitful work.

Take, for example, a group of pupils which has agreed to make a tape
recording about a collection of poems. It is instructive to look at what may
happen in such a situation. The teacher may well have to restrain himself:
the pupils may seem to be getting nowhere, and a great deal of time may be
spent in seemingly fruitless false starts or in apparently unrelated, desultory
conversation. The teacher needs to hold back, resist the temptation to take
over and to carry out the task for the pupils, and let them talk their way
through it. It is perfectly proper to make individual suggestions, dropped
casually into the pool of ideas emerging from the talk. The more informally
this can be done, the better. If the teacher can manage to leave the problem
to the group and himself get on with something else, this may well be the
best thing to do—although such apparent opting-out will often be greeted
with indignation by the pupils. Although their main concerns will be with
the end-product, the real educative activity will be in the group discussions
and talk that lead to its being achieved. Other end-products, such as wall
charts, models, or anthologies, can serve similar purposes, and it is essential
to have this intended physical outcome to which the activity of the talk is
directed. It will serve as a better focus for the work than any attempt at
constant intervention by the teacher.

One of the most important things that the pupil does in this regime of
group talk is to discover new possibilities in his relationship with his teacher
... if the teacher allows it. This important discovery cannot be made unless
the teacher is prepared to stand back, avoid imposing his own suggestions,
and wait for the pupil to ask. The teacher's very status gives his suggestions
such weight that they impose themselves unless the pupil can consider them
alongside other suggestions. Those trained in the traditional mould will find
this detachment of themselves difficult, but even the best of us tend to teach
too much and prepare too little. If we set out to have the pupil do as much as
possible without our regular intervention, we have to reorientate the whole
relationship between what we ourselves do in class and what we do beforehand.

Talking with others

The pupils' group talk is not of course the only kind of speaking and listening in which they need to engage. The school environment is inevitably artificial, and every opportunity should be taken to let pupils go out, generally in pairs, into the world outside the school, to talk with as many different kinds of people as possible. One of us recalls a group of pupils working on the implications for the area of the coming of the motorway link-up in the West Midlands. They went one day to talk with a group of Irish labourers on the motorway site, and the next day to have lunch with the managing director of a big firm manufacturing car components. A great deal was being learned about the social functions of talk in varying contexts, and the children were beginning to develop a repertoire of varieties or registers[1], adapting their style of speech to each particular situation.

The same principle applies to real situations which can be imported into the school. The greeting of visitors should always be in part a task for pupils, as should the process of getting visitors to work on whatever is going on in school at the moment. The last thing most children want from a visitor is a formal lecture. In the motorway project mentioned above, the local Planning Officer visited the school and was put to talking with groups of pupils about his work, and the pupils' ideas for the future of the town. One comes to recognize at once the open-ended, exploratory school which one cannot visit without being thrust into a group of questioning children, and to prefer it, as educationally better in every way, to the school where the entry of a visitor brings rows of children to their feet in deferential silence. Manning the school telephone under supervision enables children of 11 to learn how to respond to all kinds of callers, as does reception-desk duty in a busy school. The more of these genuine situations in which we can involve pupils, the more their awareness of the social roles of talking and listening will develop. In an increasingly oral society, this is vital for their future effectiveness and happiness.

Of course there will never be enough of these real situations to go round. But the Hillview Project (C. Hannam, P. Smyth, and N. Stephenson, *Young Teachers and Reluctant Learners*, Penguin) revealed the degree of alienation which can separate adolescents from their seniors. This suggests a long history of non-communication between adults and children. Schools complain about the flood of student teachers, yet miss the opportunity to give each of them a conversation group of children who are briefed to tell the newcomer all about this or that aspect of the school or the classwork— and in the process learn more than the student himself. Talk is so easily taken for granted, but is in reality a set of skills which has to be given time and space and opportunity, and is the key to most of what follows in every child's schooling.

Where real experience fails us we can fall back on role-playing, simulations, and games. A group can act out an incident, to the class or through the intermediary of the tape-recorder. Examples might be the vicar and parish council disagreeing about levelling the churchyard; a woman with three children wrongly accused of shoplifting; the local newspaper interviewing the teacher about an incident and getting it all wrong; and many more instances closer to the lives of the children. Word games should be, like role-playing activities, above all, enjoyable. One favourite is to give each pupil the names of five unlikely objects, and ask him to weave them into a story so that the rest of the class cannot spot them. There are many more suggestions for talk situations in Andrew Wilkinson's *Spoken English* (University of Birmingham) Chapter 3.

The role of talk in language learning clearly poses problems of discipline. Discipline among teachers is apt to be what religion used to be—too personal to talk about. However, many elements in this book exemplify our belief that teachers can only give their pupils freedom if they have it to give, and this implies a framework of order. The teacher who never gives a definite instruction, for fear of rupturing the precious 'relationships', has not yet in fact established relationships which *work*. The good teacher can afford to make suggestions which pupils are free to reject, because he has made clear the difference between suggestion and instruction. (It is useful here to distinguish very clearly between a class-teacher role, and a small-group-participant role. The good teacher will often symbolize this contrast bv standing up for the one role and always being seated with the group for the other.) As our command of a situation grows, we shall become free to send pairs of pupils off to carry out a task away from direct supervision, and to show in other ways the trust in our pupils which is necessary if they are to learn to be self-sufficient. The weak teacher exhibits a fear or mistrust of his pupils which they are quick to reciprocate.

One other aspect of talk and its importance in the policy of English teaching in a school should also be mentioned. Developing a diversity of gifts in the use of speech is usually better done in mixed-ability groups. These are more likely to yield a mixture of social backgrounds with different levels of language competence. It is just as important for the gifted or privileged child to learn to talk to children from more deprived homes as the reverse. For this reason, many secondary school English departments prefer mixed-ability groups in the early years, in line with the now powerful trend away from streaming in primary and middle schools.

Drama

Drama is a basic means of communication and a natural means of learning. The way young children are dramatic in much of their play is a commonplace of educational literature. Adults, too, telling a story in a relaxed situation, use gesture and imitate accents to dramatize their account. Teachers of English need to use this natural tendency to dramatize, just as they use other natural tendencies. Language itself enables us to build up in our inner mind a model of the world: we try things out verbally in imagination before trying them out in reality; we explore the courses of action open to us before choosing one. In this way language makes possible for us a number of potential worlds, and drama works in a very similar way, especially for our more complex and inter-personal relationships. Role-playing, acting out parts less or more real, enables children to explore 'What would happen if . . .?' Older pupils can prepare for crucial interviews by acting them out, playing the part of the interviewer as well as the applicant. The dramatized version can be inspected and discussed. Younger children, too, can act out situations which they have not yet experienced, and situations which are painful can be made more manageable by being re-presented: playing the part of father in a family quarrel can illuminate and extend understanding in unexpected ways.

Left to themselves to improvise drama, inexperienced pupils use hackneyed school or T.V.-serial situations. Perhaps every class has to go through this stage, and the teacher may need to be tolerant of its tedious clichés. Gradually, more structured situations can be developed, and many of these can derive from imaginative literature. The standing of literature is apt to make many inexpert teachers feel that they must needs approach it in a formal, literary way, and as has been often said, they murder to dissect. This applies to many classes up to the age of 15, whose need to engage with literature at a more than surface level is not met by methods of literary criticism. Dramatization is one obvious way toward meeting this need. For the middle years, myth and legend offer abundant scope: Beowulf or the Hercules story, re-told or read aloud with energy, can yield profound dramatization by children who play the parts and use mime or their own spontaneous dialogue. A reading of a book like Ann Holm's *I am David* (Puffin), is not interrupted by a session of acting out what might happen next: it is enriched and the children's grasp of character and plot is deepened. Such dramatic exploration offers material for discussion of why an author wrote what he did at some point, and already the class is engaging with literature seriously. One might add that a book's capacity to sustain this kind of exploration is a useful index of its value both as literature and as language. Much the same holds for ballads and narrative poetry of similar kinds—not only the well-tried ones like 'Sir Patrick Spens', but comic ballads like 'Get up and Bar the Door!' (both in A.F. Scott, *Poems for Pleasure*, Book I, C.U.P.) and modern folk ballads, all of which lend themselves to improvisation and mime to accompany a reading.

Schools vary a great deal in their organization of drama work. Some have drama lessons timetabled with a specialist teacher, and this can be an asset when the work is integrated with the work of an English department whose strengths lie elsewhere. But lack of special training is no bar to making intelligent use of L.E.A. courses or the specialist handbooks written on the subject[2]. We would rather see every English specialist disposed to experiment with drama than ask that every school have a drama specialist. But there does need to be a clear understanding of what drama is all about. It is first of all an opportunity for children to explore and develop their own physical potential and awareness, to become aware of their own bodies and how they communicate, and to extend the social skills. Adolescents who are insensitive to the way they barge through crowded corridors, for example, have at some point missed a vital lesson about themselves. The heightening of self-awareness that mime and role-playing can bring about is valuable in itself. For English teaching it is valuable because many children develop imaginative awareness more quickly through physical activity than through the use of words. In a sense drama can provide some of the basic experiences which language can only represent in symbolic form. To aim·first at the verbal representation may short-circuit a vital element in the experience of many less articulate pupils. In this respect drama offers a potent extension to history and religious education teachers, too. Apart from literature, there are several other possible starting points:

1. *A dressing-up box*. This should usually be quite simple; even a bag full of old hats can be enough. The garments in the box will suggest characters to the children, who can be asked to form groups and make up plays in which the characters figure. We have seen many children who can exhibit the kind of eerie genius in clowning with simple objects that one associates with Chaplin or the Marx Brothers (whose sequence trying to get off a boat in *Monkey Business* is a wonderful example to show to children).

2. *A props box.* Take an object as simple as a large flannel scarf, or a length of heavy rope, and ask pupils to explore as many different uses as they can think of. A walking-stick will serve as a gun, a fishing rod, a strongman's iron bar, an oar, a toasting fork, and several dozen more. One is often surprised, and humbled, by what 'remedial' pupils can produce in this kind of work.

3. *Tape-recordings.* Drama work can be based on responses to sounds. Put together a series of unusual sounds, have the class guess what they are, and suggest they make a dramatized story which brings all of them in. (This stimulus is useful for writing, too, but the drama work is a good preparation.) Groups can be asked to make a tape telling a story entirely in sounds, and this can in turn generate in less able children a new responsiveness to sound.

4. *Situations taken by the teacher from books*, used in drama as preparation for studying them. We have seen adolescents in an approved school (as it then was) setting up a training-session on shoplifting, and finding their later discussion of Fagin in Dickens' *Oliver Twist* altogether more challenging than they would otherwise have done.

5. *Everyday experience.* Children's daily diaries ought to have moved out of the home by the age of 9, and should have ceased to be daily. This will be eased if they are asked to record events that they see happening. If they do, the recording of them will yield many episodes for drama work—a squabble over jumping a bus-queue, a scene over an alleged theft from a market stall, the behaviour of their adolescent seniors, and much else.

6. *Places.* J.S. Bruner's now celebrated work, *Man, A Course of Study* (Curriculum Development Associates) includes films of Eskimo life and suggests related drama work. Pupils mark out the floor of an igloo and work out just how they would sleep eight people in such a small space—an exploration through the physical senses once again. Deprived and even average children who lack this kind of physical experience in the middle years may later find imaginative response to more abstract experience very difficult. One of the most fertile of all places for exploring in this way, as the Opies have shown, is the school playground itself.[3]

Throughout this discussion of drama we have avoided reference to theatre. The distinction between the two is important: theatre implies an activity in which the presence of an audience is paramount, whereas drama, with or without an audience, is done for its own sake rather than for the observer's. The younger the children, the more the existence or needs of an audience should be played down. If a primary or middle school must go in for performances, let it be done through a theatre club or workshop. The teacher needing advice on organizing such a club should read Robert Leach's book on the subject, *Theatre for Youth* (Pergamon).

The line of development which drama work follows in the top years of the middle school and beyond is directed only very obliquely towards theatre, if at all. The pupils come to engage with written plays, it is true, although few children can benefit from this before the age of 13. But without the prior experience of unscripted drama, and in all too many cases with it, children are pushed into work with written plays as a purely literary activity which does not touch the stage at any point. Teachers have done and still do great damage by this, especially to Shakespeare. But to interpret a dramatic text needs a skilled eye for how the printed score will look and sound and feel when performed—and the analogy with interpreting music is not accidental. If there is a proper transitional stage between improvised and scripted drama, it should not be before the third year of secondary school, and one of us has prepared a set of appropriate texts for precisely this transition (Anthony Adams and Robert Leach, *Drama Action*, Blackie).

Chapter 5

Reading

We have dealt with talking, listening, and drama before coming to reading, and have done so deliberately in spite of the widespread assumption that reading is the first objective of English teaching. We have done this in order to reflect linguistic realities: spoken language is prior to written, and some distinguished experts have been utterly wrong in thinking that children obtain their first knowledge of linguistic structures from their reading. Beyond this, however, reading is not so much a body of knowledge as a set of skills. It is also a set of skills which can go on being acquired and refined throughout one's school career and beyond it. There is a sense in which the English teacher is never *not* teaching reading. By the same token, the English teacher may have to cope with defects in reading at a quite elementary level. For example, one of us taught a sixth-form group in which a student had never mastered where English uses a doubled consonant, and it was necessary to take him back to the methods used in the infant school, teach some basic word recognition, and insist on some rote-learning of key spellings. It does nothing for such a student if we complain, merely, that the junior school has not done its job.

There are sound reasons, which we explain more fully in Chapter 8, for expecting any class of 9 year olds to include a number of children, possibly a substantial number, who cannot yet read adequately. In sharp contrast to this, many teachers of upper juniors expect their pupils to have reached this stage, and feel ill-equipped to cope with those who have not done so. One very serious consequence is that teachers become very anxious, and only too easily communicate their anxiety to the children. By now the whole business of 'teaching reading' has become invested with an aura of concern which can have good and bad effects. If colleges of education are led to take their responsibilities in this field far more seriously than in the past, this will be a good effect. If teachers of juniors and younger secondary classes set out to learn some of the necessary technicalities of teaching reading, this, too, will be a good effect. But if teachers generally acquire the impression that reading is something that can 'be taught' and, once taught, can be assumed to endure, or to develop spontaneously, the effects may be bad.

Reading is like any other complex set of skills in resisting all attempts to 'teach' it in a rapid, decisive, or final manner. It is well to remind ourselves of the complexity of the skills involved in reading: learning to use a typewriter at high speed is simplicity itself by comparison. But learning to read is very much like learning to use a typewriter in that the outcome of the whole process is a secondary rather than a primary educational attainment—reading is a means rather than an end in itself. The anxiety-ridden attempt to make reading an end in itself, which bedevils many classrooms, is one of the main sources of the unhappiness which the whole business produces in many children. At the same time, there are too many children in most classes aged 9 or 10 who cannot yet read well for the teacher to rely on the remedial specialist or on withdrawal groups to do the job. Very many children of this age, and older ones, still need positive help with reading but do not qualify for remedial help.[1] The reading attainment of a class will reflect much more than what is done specifically about reading skills. The whole curriculum of children of this age needs to be thought of as a reading-supportive environment.

Approaches to reading

Reading methods
There has been a long controversy about methods and media in the teaching of reading, which we do not propose to enter into. The teacher who wishes to pursue it more fully can find a cool-headed and well-informed survey in Donald Moyle's *The Teaching of Reading* (3rd edn., Ward Lock), probably the best short book on the subject. Like many other educational controversies those about reading have been characterized by disputes between approaches which should be viewed as complementary rather than competitive. Some have claimed a superiority which later evidence or experience has not supported.

Some approaches to reading frankly misconceive the nature of language itself. For example, claims have been made for what are known technically as Special Writing Systems, the best known of which is the Initial Teaching Alphabet. The basis of these claims is the alleged muddle and confusion of English orthography, but some recent research studies suggest that English spelling is by no means as muddled as has been thought (see Chapter 8, pp.108 f.). This will seem a slender counterweight to the voluminous

studies which have been devoted to the relative merits of the various
approaches. However, the status of 'research' itself is easily misconstrued,
and the number of variables which affect the findings of any investigation
is very great. Investigations in the field of educational research have
usually sustained the views of the researcher and we are led to be somewhat
sceptical about the kind of activity which passes for 'research'. The only
matter on which researchers appear to agree is that children learn what
they are taught—and that teachers who believe in their methods are more
successful than those with less commitment. So far as current knowledge
can tell us, the attitudes of the teacher will make a greater difference to
the children's learning than will the use of a particular method. The teacher
who has a choice of method is likely to succeed more.

Almost all teaching of reading in the past has rested on the use of a
reading scheme. Just what 'scheme' may mean in this context is very debat-
able. We now know that the grading claimed for very many so-called reading
schemes is quite spurious. The earliest basis for this grading was word-counts,
and whether the counts are based on children's speech, or on frequencies in
the standard language, or on another source, makes little difference:
a reading scheme based on a limited or 'controlled' vocabulary *alone* is
bound to distort the language actually used, most notably in producing a
forced style and an artificial syntax. The result is a language more or less
totally divorced from the spoken language of the children who are to use it.
The vast majority of 'simplified' writing intended for use in reading schemes
is simplified only in respect of vocabulary, but its authors have been quite
unaware of the complexity of the syntax they expect children to understand.
Arguably, in any case, children's reading experience should include many of
the so-called difficulties rather than try to protect readers from them. (For
examples of syntactic traps of this sort, see J. Reid, *Reading, Problems and
Practices*, Ward Lock, pp.394—403.)

The use of word counting to limit the length of sentences is similarly
suspect. To illustrate the point, this sentence could be written more simply:
'There is something wrong, too, about using the number of words in each
sentence as an indication of the difficulty of a piece of reading.' The second
version may be clearer, but is very much longer. On a word-count basis it
would be more difficult rather than less. This is a very naive view of textual
difficulty. There have been many more sophisticated attempts to assess the
difficulty of texts. These have usually emerged in 'readability formulae',
nearly all of which employ number-of-words-per-sentence as one element,
and the frequency of individual words as another. The truth is that all
readability formulae must be inadequate, because language is not formulaic.

The best way of measuring readability is the use of 'cloze' procedure: children are provided with texts in which one word in five or one word in ten is blanked out, and they are asked to guess or work out the missing items. This method gives results which reflect the difficulty which actual children have with actual books. But, and it is a very important but, 'cloze' procedures will give results not much more accurate than those obtained by an experienced teacher judging in the light of her own classes. This was confirmed by the discovery that a carefully-written reading scheme which meets many of the objections made in this chapter (the Griffin books and Dragon books, published by E.J. Arnol and written by S. McCullagh) was shown by 'cloze' procedure to have its books in the right order and mainly with the right gradations. (See Donald Mo 'Readability' in J. Merritt, *Reading and the Curriculum*, Ward Lock.)

Even the best reading scheme, however, is quite insufficient on its own, and is grossly insufficient if it is abandoned too soon. Many children are allowed to 'go off' the reading scheme when they reach a reading age of 9 years. This is almost certainly too soon, and if there is no other curricular attack on reading it is too soon by at least two years of reading age. The reason for this is that a reading age score is a very bad index of genuine reading competence. If children are to come to read well enough to enjoy it and to do it at their ease, they need an infinitely higher attainment than the 9 year old reading age. There are many children, too, who are happier with the support of the reading scheme until the books in it are all but identical with the books in the class or school library. This sustained use of a schematic approach to reading also helps the teacher in keeping track of where the children have got to—although a bare reading age score and a list of books read will not make anything like a sufficient record of children's reading attainment. It would seem to follow that a reading scheme, in the proper sense of the term, is not a single sequence of books published by one firm for one author, but a whole library of such graded books, collected and organized by a teacher interested and well-informed enough to undertake the task. Sticking loyally by a single 'scheme' is false economy, even if it is thought to be the 'best'.

Specific techniques

In the 9 to 13 age range we are more likely to encounter children who have tried to learn to read and failed than we are with younger children. There is a danger here, which is insufficiently guarded against in many schools, that methods and devices conceived for remedial purposes may become part of the permanent routine of the pupils. To take one very well known instance, one of the S.R.A. Reading Laboratories has been shown to produce quite remarkable gains in reading attainment with under-achieving children of 11 and 12, in a very few months. What is less well known is that the continued use of such laboratories after these gains have been achieved is of much less benefit to the children. These Reading Laboratories are firmly grounded in learning psychology and are written with considerable skill, but they are *remedial* devices. Precisely the same is true of the Ward Lock Reading Laboratories, which are much less like their American counterparts than they look. (The difficulties created by American spellings in the S.R.A. laboratories are of course minimal; the British ones may be preferred, but there are better reasons than this.)

Among other remedial materials of considerable value with very retarded readers of 12 and 13 we should mention D.H. Stott's *Programmed Reading Kit* (Holmes MacDougall). It is not, and cannot be, anything like as tightly programmed as its title would imply, but it was originally devised specifically for remedial purposes. It calls for careful study before use, and the teacher should not expect miracles from any single resource. Most useful to the ordinary teacher in this situation, probably, is the *approach* adopted in the teaching material *Breakthrough to Literacy* (Longman) by D. Mackay, B. Thompson, and P. Schaub. This is not a reading scheme in any sense but does offer a way of making full use, in reading work, of the vocabulary and meanings the pupils wish to use. (For a lucid description, see D. Mackay, 'Breakthrough to Literacy' in J. Merritt, *Reading and the Curriculum*, Ward Lock.) It stands in complete contrast to workbooks based on slot-and-filler exercises, which are limiting and stultifying in the worst degree. The best-known of these, by Ronald Ridout (published by Ginn and Co.) have little theoretical basis in either psychological or linguistic respects, are seriously out of date, and in some respects mislead their users.

The language environment
The reading achievements of a class are radically affected by the pupils' mastery of word-recognition skills, it is true. But they will reflect much more than this, if there is much more to reflect. This brings us to the 'reading-supportive environment' which we have mentioned earlier. If every activity of the classroom may bear on reading and require it, let this fact be exploited to the full. By a supportive environment we mean, first of all, one in which many people are reading, and enjoying it; where reading is constantly helped and lack of success is not met with punishment or verbal

chastisement; where the teacher hears the children read as regularly as they need[2], and where the children hear the teacher read, too. A reading-supportive environment will include broadcasts and films which relate to books to be found in the classroom. The books themselves will be found in the classroom, not tucked tightly on shelves with barely legible spines outward, but displayed where the fronts can be seen. The environment will include visits to the local library, and, just as important, to and from the children's librarian. There should be stories read by the teacher, and some read by the children; some of them read 'live', some of them on tape or (better) cassette, and some on records. There should be language games, too: just because Scrabble or Lexicon are party games in middle class homes is no reason for regarding them as superfluous in classrooms of deprived children.

Books and stories and the rest of the classroom's resources are only part of the environment, and for many children a rather inert part. There are other uses of written language all about them which should be exploited. Common advertisements, television leads and captions, road signs, shop names, brand labels, the games on the backs of cereal packets, programmes in the *Radio Times*, even the daily papers and the names and addresses of people in the school—all of these things are real, and children relate to them. Teachers can exploit them as objects bearing labels in written language, to form a first element in what we are calling an exploitative view of the reading curriculum. These things are a first element: drills and skills are means to these objects and their labels, and hence come second. This does not imply that word-recognition does not matter. Once again the need is not for one or other but for both.

An exploitative reading curriculum, in the sense in which we have used the term, sets out to engage the pupils in activities and inquiries which both relate to their everyday lives and entail the use of written language, and in particular entail interpreting a text. The conscious inclusion of a language-using element in every activity thus runs parallel to our conscious inclusion of elements which use the four language activities in the examples of work-cards and worksheets given in this book. The list of letters written by a single class (see p.79) is a more concrete example of the exploitative approach moving beyond the classroom and being carried much further.

Reading 'theory'

Non-specialists who ask experienced colleagues about the teaching of
reading quickly find themselves confused by the jargon, which is used by
teachers who, like most of us, object strenuously to jargon in others.
'Phonics', 'look and say', 'flash cards', and many other terms fill the air.
The methods referred to will be advocated with dogmatic enthusiasm or
mentioned with a hesitant lack of commitment, and in either case the
seeker after guidance feels doubtful about the advice. At the research
level, too, a close inspection of prevailing methods, of research studies
designed to evaluate them, and of the theories behind them, has led us to
conclude that nobody really *knows* what happens when children learn to
read. The available expertise has tended to concentrate on evaluating
particular methods, sometimes from previously committed positions,
rather than on looking closely at the cognitive operations involved.
However, this has begun to change.

'Phonics' is a generic label for the approach which requires children to
learn the correspondences between the sounds of the spoken language (or
some of them) and the symbols of the written one (or some of them).
British practice has now outgrown the teaching of the traditional names
of the letters, and teaches the main sound-equivalance of each symbol.
Most phonic approaches deal with most or all of the 44 basic sounds of
the language, but they vary enormously in how far they cater for the
corresponding symbols, which in reality run to several hundred. The
usage of written English in practice relies very heavily on about 160. But
teachers who use 'phonics' are apt to deal with only 50 or 60 of these.
(See Frank Smith, 'The Efficiency of Phonics', in Frank Smith, (ed.)
Psycholinguistics and Reading, Holt, Rinehart, and Winston.) The
difficulty of making a phonic approach exhaustive can be seen by looking
at the symbols which can correspond to the same sound in a single instance:
height, eye, I, bite, right, isle, buy, by, died, dyed, indict, and two or three
more. Nevertheless, many children have learned to read very successfully
in a system relying on phonics, and their success has therefore been
attributed to the method. But we have known for half a century that when
the first phase of learning to read has passed, children do not identify words
they know by identifying the individual letters in them. It is not physically
possible to identify the letters and to read as fast as most children soon
come to do. For this reason, phonics has serious limitations, and the ap-
roach is inherently less efficient than most of its users suppose. Moreover
there is a good deal of linguistic nonsense talked about 'blends'. These are
simply two-letter or three-letter symbols.

'Look and say' is a label for an approach to reading which for many years was regarded as being in competition with phonics. It started from the accurate perception that children do not long stop to identify individual letters, and proceeded to require children to learn the profiles of common words. One of the more common ways of doing this was (and is) the use of 'flash cards' which show one word at a time. Unfortunately, the words most often used have profiles which fit a great many words, and the flash card offers no clue to the child about which word it may be except those provided by the individual symbols—i.e. the phonic clues. The exclusive reliance of some schools on 'look and say' is bound to cause some serious gaps in pupils' knowledge about how symbols correspond to sounds, and these gaps emerge in the later years of the secondary school, if not earlier, as major weaknesses of spelling. It will be evident that 'look and say' is both efficient and inefficient, just as 'phonics' are, but that the strengths and weaknesses of the two are complementary. Rather less widely used is a 'whole sentence' approach, which relies on short, simple sentences to be read in the immediate context of pictures which provide accurate clues to the reading. The strength of this approach is that it recognizes the inherent continuousness of language: reading is, indeed, much more than decoding separate words. Its weakness is precisely that it may instil a notion of the sentence which is much too short and simplistic to be of use in the practical functions of language. Here again, the approach fits in well as one element among others.

All these approaches to reading, like those which rely on special alphabets, are rapidly falling into some disrepute among well-informed scholars, but they are so well established in the publishers' catalogues and school stock-rooms that they will be with us for a long time to come. The disfavour with which experts view them stems from two sources. If there is one, abiding lesson of educational research, it is that a method is as good as the devotion of its user—and in reading, many teachers tend to be the prisoners of their method rather than its masters. At a more serious level, all these approaches are based on a learning theory which evolved before the immense growth in our understanding of language that has taken place since the mid-1950s. Since reading is a process of responding to written language, the nature of language itself, and of written text in particular, would seem to be essential elements in an adequate theory of reading. These elements are only now beginning to be explored fully, by specialists working in the field rather sadly known as psycholinguistics. It would be a pity if teachers allowed the label of this important field of study to put them off its findings, some of which enable us to predict the direction in which reading theory is likely to change in the next decade or so—and it does seem certain that a major re-orientation is coming.[3]

To summarize our expectations very briefly and crudely, we must expect a vastly greater appreciation of the role of a child's existing knowledge of his own language, and of the world about him. We would expect numerous studies to show that a child's fluency as a talker before he tries to learn to read will markedly affect how successful he is at reading. We should expect, too, a greater understanding of the role of contextual clues in any reading process, and a more detailed awareness of the many ways in which written language, just because it is written, is unlike spoken language. This general development can also be expected to show the linguistic and the psychological study of language and reading adopting much more similar positions than in the past. One aspect of this is already apparent: specialists in reading have widely accepted the view that spoken and written language are different but in their own domains equal. It will no longer do to regard one as inferior to the other. They are also in the process of accepting that it is unreal to expect children to learn to handle written language from a spoken language environment. But the contrast between spoken and written, while important, is not an opposition, and we have stressed the value of constantly building bridges between them in school.

One bridge which we would not advocate, however, is that which is sometimes called sub-vocal talking, or 'sub-vocalization'. There are some children, and there are some stages in learning to read, where sub-vocalization has a useful part to play. But normal children rapidly outgrow it, and should be encouraged to do so. The child who does all his reading by sub-vocalizing it, as it were reading it aloud quietly to himself, is bound to be reading very slowly. (At the other extreme, the adult who never does it at all is likely, on occasion, to miss important elements in complicated texts.) One implication of this for middle school teaching is that children whose teacher no longer hears them read need to be given tasks involving some reading aloud, but with the emphasis on the meaning of the text as a whole rather than on individual words. Many British experts would go further and say that the boundary between reading as a subject and reading as a frequent and natural classroom activity should be broken down as soon as possible. This would imply much less use of 'reading schemes' and much more use of schemes of work in which reading has to happen, together with far more interaction between school and the world outside school (even if only with other schools).

The reader who has turned to this section looking for definitive answers

to his problems may feel that he has been given the dustiest answer of all—
that there are no answers. In practice, however, if he will absorb the caution we suggest about rigid advocacy of any single approach, and can per-
suade an experienced colleague to let him see the teaching of initial literacy
going on, he will be able to see for himself the two over-riding realities: the
teaching of reading is a long, slow, complex process, and the variety of
approaches that is available offers a fair chance of being able to help
struggling pupils, provided the non-specialist teacher is not expected to
handle the problem unaided.

Hearing children read

What precisely is meant by this central activity in 'teaching reading'? The
class's work has to be organized so that the pupils who need a period of
undivided attention from the teacher can have it regularly. The pupils who
are to be heard should come to the teacher in ones or twos, ready to read
from a text which both the pupil and the teacher can see without difficulty. The rest of the class should not be in a position to attend closely
to what the teacher is doing. When children read to the teacher, they
should not be in the position of candidates trying to pass a test: the
teacher should watch for the difficulties and help the child over them,
rather than watch for the errors and pounce on them. The particular
elements that the teacher watches for will vary from child to child. With
one there will be recognition problems, and listing other examples can
often help the learning. With another the word-recognition is well developed but there is little sense of the shape of a sentence: here the reading
may be punctuated by 'Let's take that bit through again and get the full
sense of it.' With yet another the reading may be fluent, but the child may
not in fact understand more than a fraction of what he has read, and a
quite different response is called for. In each case the activity is a co-
operative one, but a great many teachers find it a strain. There is an enduring temptation, as there was in the old practice of reading round the class,
to let the child who most needs a relatively long practice get away with a
very short one. Indeed, some specialists in reading have speculated that
the amount of time given to each child's reading to the teacher may have
more to do with success in learning to read than any other factor. If this
were true, and there is no reason at present to deny it, the explanation
would be that children who are called up to read only one page of text at
a time have too strong a temptation to learn each page by heart, and too
little incentive to practise and master the mechanisms of scanning and
speaking different segments simultaneously. However, the part played by

the teacher in hearing children read is not that of a merely passive hearer, and a very great deal of the learning that can take place in these small individual sessions is lost if the teacher does not play a very active and responsive role.

What children read

The supply of books

The teacher's biggest contribution throughout the 9 to 13 age range is in reading aloud to his pupils. For many children, even quite able ones, narrative is difficult to read with any full meaning. They can register the sense of the text, perhaps, but cannot transpose it into any kind of 'internal performance'. Children who are used to being read to at home are usually those who most quickly learn to read for themselves, so the support of good reading aloud is relevant to all children. The teacher's second great contribution is in saturating his pupils with books: books to read, to look at, to get information from; childish books to revert to; difficult technical books to puzzle out; large books of fine pictures to wonder at. And this large, expensive, vastly diverse stock of books is in its right place on desks and tables, on display racks and windowsills. Neatly ranged ranks of undisturbed library books are idle capital, producing only self-esteem in their keeper. If the school signals to children that library books are something special, or that reading is 'outside reading', the children will get the message, and their antipathy to reading will be exactly what the school deserves.

More and more, the books which make the classroom a bookroom are paperbacks. This is as it should be. In terms of what each reading of a book costs, paperbacks are about half as expensive as hardbacks. Children identify with them readily, and it is brute fact that there is more good contemporary children's literature in paperback form than in hardback. Their lack of durability, too, may be more of a virtue than appears at first sight. If a junior school rightly buys six copies of six titles nowadays, where it used to buy a class set of one title, the wear and tear on them enforces a re-appraisal of the stock cupboard that most schools could carry out with profit. A paperback stock ought to be replaced in the course of three years in any case, with a sensitive eye to the changing scene in children's literature, and to its 'packaging', which can strongly affect a book's appeal. For all these reasons, too, it seems unprofitable to think of re-binding paperbacks in hard covers.

Children judge books very quickly. They look at the blurb, or the opening page, or the illustrations, or, more commonly, the length, and if any of these meets with disapproval they reach for the label most ready to hand—'boring'. Moreover, one of the yardsticks that children use here is whether a book resembles a textbook. If it does, its prospects are not good. This is why the book-jackets on trade or 'net' books are valuable, and the polythene sleeves for covering them even more so. But even more precious than the dust-jacket is ownership. There are a number of commercial organizations which supply books for re-sale, and school bookshops are now authorized by the Publishers Association under the Book Agency Scheme, which can benefit the school financially. Such bookshops, while they can be run by parents, need the supervision of a teacher in selecting the stock. They may also be the only place in a neighbourhood which offers a reasonable variety of children's books, and they can thus be very valuable to parents as well as pupils. (For further information, write to The Publishers Association, 19 Bedford Square, London WC1B 3HJ, or the school's nearest retail bookseller.)

Alongside a large amount of reading aloud by the teacher and much individual reading by the children, there needs also to be more intensive reading. The objective of this is a dual one: to bring children to a closer understanding of how good authors use words, and to make quite sure of the imaginative enrichment that worthwhile literature can provide. The practice of reading round the class is a quite deplorable substitute for intensive reading as we understand it. What we mean by intensive reading can best be illustrated by two examples.

Group reading

Reading is a solitary activity, and school as a public place is ill-suited to it. Beside this paradox lies another: the main way of resolving the problem, group reading, has been more widely used with younger juniors, where it is often quite unhelpful, than with the 9 to 13 range where it can be really useful. To ask the halting reader of 7 to read aloud to his group is to depress the morale and attainment of the whole group: such work should be reserved until children can read with at least moderate fluency. Too often children go from reading badly to a group to reading even more badly to a whole class, and the difficulty of finding books which suit a mixed-ability class accentuates the problem. On a sound basis, however, group reading in the middle years can be very valuable indeed. The teacher should have access to a stockroom containing sets of six or seven copies of each of a wide

variety of titles, so that each group can be equipped wi'h a book appropriate to its attainment. Each book should be supplied with a worksheet
suggesting a range of activities—dramatizing this part, making a tape of
that, writing about personal experiences analogous to those in the book,
looking at its situations through the eyes of different characters, and so on.

Setting up worksheets of this kind requires the teacher to read the available books with some care, but Heinemann Educational have now issued a
series of Reading Study Units related to a dozen or so titles in the New
Windmill Library, which are good examples of this approach. Each of these
four-page leaflets gives information about book and author, and a series
of activities for individual and group work. They have been based on the
known successes of the list, but even the best commercially produced
worksheets are no substitute for those made by the teacher himself for his
own pupils, partly because classwork on a book needs to include discussion
with a teacher who has read it thoroughly. Even so, there are novels which
resemble poems in being better treated as material for group reading that
calls for no further exploration afterwards.

The short story

Intensive reading becomes difficult if the work being read goes on so long
that children lose its thread. The short story avoids this problem, and also
does less damage if it proves to have been a mistaken selection. The kind of
worksheet treatment already suggested is easier to develop and offers the
teacher a chance to experiment and learn from errors. Harrap's *Storymakers*
and Blackie's Globe Short Story Library cater specifically for teachers of
children in the middle years. Short stories are best bought in 'half sets' of
about twenty copies, so that all pupils can follow a reading by sharing a
copy. A common pattern is for the teacher to read a story aloud while the
pupils follow, and to move into discussion of theme, plot, character, or
whatever aspect exercises the pupils' mind. This is followed by written work
on a related theme. The only thing wrong with this pattern is a tendency for
teachers to use it without variation. It is banal, for instance, to invite children
to write on the theme of a story so brilliant as James Thurber's 'The Night
the Ghost Got In' (in *Thurber Carnival*, Penguin): the pupil will be too much
influenced by the model to write for himself, and the model is far too
difficult to emulate. Such a story is better treated as one of several illustrations
of a theme.

Even with children of 9, however, there is a place for some literary study.
We would most firmly oppose any sort of literary critical approach, except
perhaps with gifted children of 11 and upwards. Questions which seek to

distance the reader from the story are bound to confuse many children: they should be focusing on the story and its meaning rather than on their feelings and whether those feelings are 'true' to the story. Rather, the teacher should ask children to explore the possibilities of converting a story into other media, tape or drama, chat-show interviews with leading characters, wordless drawings to tell the key episodes, and so on. At a more mature level it is feasible to juxtapose different stories with similar themes and examine the treatment of the central ideas. Alternatively one can take a story narrated by one character and have it re-told by another. It is in these oblique ways that children come to appreciate that a literary artefact is something made, rather than something that 'just happens'.

The class reader

A few years ago English specialists led a determined swing away from using the same book with a whole class at a time, and the pendulum now seems to be swinging back again. The more diverse the English work of a class becomes, and the more it employs group methods, the more valuable it will be to have a bare minimum of material that everybody knows. The non-specialist is also likely to have to use a class reader because that is what the school makes available. The list of books in Sources and Resources II will be useful if the teacher can make any choice among the stock, but whether he has a 'good read' or not, he should avoid using it for 'reading round the class'. The good reader gains little by it, and the bad reader is harmed. The good reader has finished the book long before the class as a whole, while the slow reader will lose the narrative thread unless it is used every period until the book is finished. Once again, large parts of it should be read by the teacher. Large parts of it, too, should be read silently: for children who have never experienced it, thirty minutes of silent reading can be a novel experience and not at first an easy one. Other parts may be apportioned for *prepared* reading by groups of children: a group can be given a chapter, with a leader appointed to allocate parts and run a rehearsal, dividing up the conversations and adapting the narrative passages. Such work can be recorded on tape, too, with sound effects and the like. (We have seen classes of 12 year olds turn J.R.R. Tolkien's *The Hobbit* (Allen and Unwin) into a musical, with lyrics and score written by the pupils.) All of these approaches are designed to bring the children back to the book again and again, exploring beyond the narrative line all the time.

What has been said of the short story applies to a lesser degree to the the novel, but there is much less room for manoeuvre with the class reader which is non-fiction. With a novel it is best to 'get through' the book as quickly as possible: any loss of particular words and meanings is more than compensated by the gain in impact, and the same holds for scripted plays. One of us has watched a class of 9 years olds devote an afternoon to E.B. White's *Charlotte's Web* (Puffin): nine groups of four children each took a chapter, previously allocated by the teacher, and handled it in whatever way they chose, within the prescribed limit of ten minutes for each group's presentation. In this instance, thirty of them had read it individually, mostly at home, and the decision to 'do' the whole book was made by the class. There had been six copies, along with six of each of nine other books, and it may be that their interest would have been less if it had been a class reader in the ordinary sense. Not surprisingly, the teacher's birthday was marked by a cake inscribed 'Some teacher'. (Some variations on the use of the class reader can be found in K. Calthrop, *Reading Together*, Heinemann.)

It is especially in a mixed-ability class that the library of small sets of varied books becomes very useful. Since attainment and personal maturity do not necessarily go together, the teacher using a library approach must expect some surprises. However, he can also exploit the class's rapidly growing knowledge of the books available to them. The talk about books that marks a class where reading for pleasure is normal can be a potent stimulus to previously reluctant readers, especially in overcoming the belief that reading for information is the serious business while reading fiction is a frill. This attitude is often derived from parents who identify fiction with comics and condemn all alike—a position not entirely absent, unfortunately, from staff-rooms. In attacking this prejudice, television and film can be a valuable ally, partly because they can give children the overall picture of what a novel is about, and do it better than any teacher. To dismiss all television and film as corrupting is a Luddite posture whose moral virtue is its own but nobody else's reward. In particular, a novel in a visual medium can register with different age groups in very different ways.

Consider for example the film recently made of E. Nesbit's *The Railway Children*. Girls of 9 will see this as costume drama. Boys of that age see it as a story about quaint trains. But boys of 13 and girls of that age will identify with the older girl or with Mother's problems. Very few children in this age range are going to be bothered by the sentiment in the story. At a quite different level, one of us watched a teacher of an able second year class of grammar school girls make fine use of the televised version of Jane Austen's *Sense and Sensibility*. Unaware that it was coming, the class had read the book because it was on the departmental syllabus, and had been quite reasonably bored by the apparent lack of incident. They had largely missed the irony and incisiveness of Jane Austen's dialogue, but as viewers the class readily saw how Elinor's devastating invective against Willoughby needed rare technical skill in the actress, and how much more there was in the text than they had realized.

Although we have been concerned with the reading of prose fiction, reading for information is also an important concern of English teaching. There is likely to be less resistance from some pupils to this kind of reading, and the English teacher needs to encourage and to extend the expectations of his pupils so that they do not always expect books to contain information or to be 'true'. Much that goes on in school reinforces the idea that books are repositories of 'facts'. The English teacher may need to lead his pupils to realize that there are other kinds of truth.

Chapter 6

Writing

English, however we divide it up, remains a unity. Our pages about listening and talking and reading have strayed naturally into writing, and this chapter will stray the other way. To give writing a separate chapter is only a convenience. If it is distinct from the other three elements in English, it is so not in importance but in its sheer difficulty.

We have already noted how difficult it is to read aloud. One has to utter one chunk of a text, process a second, decode the symbols of a third, and scan a fourth chunk, all at the same moment. The act of writing, dissected in the same way, appears infinitely more complicated still. Yet it is on our pupils' performance as writers that most teachers of English are judged. There was once a boy of 15 months who never spoke. His anxious grandmother claimed roundly that he had no language powers. But one day his uncle took the boy to his grandmother and gave him a series of instructions, verbally, which he most accurately obeyed. 'If he has no language,' asked the uncle, 'how does he understand my instructions?' Most employers and teachers judge the language competence of our pupils in a similarly selective way: a pupil who cannot write is liable to be adjudged illiterate. So, too, a pupil's written deficiencies glare more tellingly than any others. It is as though the taken-for-granted quality of being able to write makes people the more shocked by the absence of that skill. We have seen a backlash about 'standards', which we believe to be only beginning. Teachers in further education are exercised over endless prosings in non-sentences by their students. The trainers of teachers are baffled by the spelling and punctuation of their trainees. These consumers of our output may forget the huge scale of the change wrought by two generations, but there is not much merit in denying a charge so patently true: many students cannot spell or write as lucidly as they should. The employer and the don often fail to see that if they themselves do not hand back the mis-spelled or ill-written text for re-writing, they put the school English teacher in the exposed position of being the only purist in a lax world. For teachers of other subjects in school this silent betrayal is a less pardonable dereliction, to which we return in Chapter 9.

Some 9 year olds are, by definition, still non-readers. The proportion who are not yet writers must naturally be somewhat higher. There will be some whole classes, and many pupils, who at this age still need sustained practice in pattern-drawing, drills in the shaping of letter symbols, instruction and training in holding and using a pencil or pen (not, for immature writers, a ballpoint). Even so, most people probably ask their 9 year old pupils to write too much, and to do it too quickly. It is not hard to assess this, by collecting a single pupil's written output for a given school week and displaying it—though the teachers should agree to refrain from comment to their pupils. In schools where this rare and revealing exercise has occurred, the staff have grasped that the school's standards in writing are every teacher's responsibility, and that its demands can easily be excessive. The variety of styles and purposes in the writing is often extraordinary. It raises at once the whole question of what language in general, and written language in particular, is for.

Uses of language

There have been two useful and complementary attempts to answer this question. Working form a general view of language in its social context, Professor M.A.K. Halliday (in *Explorations in the Functions of Language*, Edward Arnold, Chapter 1) suggests that children come to realize, in practice rather than explicitly, seven uses or functions of language. Each of these has a technical label, but they are simple enough.

1. For getting things done (the 'instrumental' function).
2. For getting people to act as one wishes ('regulatory').
3. For getting on with people and groups ('interactional').
4. For expressing, discovering, or defining one's identity ('personal').
5. For finding things out ('heuristic').
6. For inventing, pretending, making fantasies ('imaginative').
7. For conveying information and describing reality ('representational').

Most readers will have no difficulty in identifying concrete examples of each of these in the talk of children of 11 and 12. Of course, no child ever views language in this detached way, and no actual use of language constitutes an example of one and only one of these functions. Any particular use of language may embody more than one. But as a catalogue it is useful, especially in helping us to notice which functions have become part of a child's spoken competence but are not yet evident in his writing. For example, the regulatory function calls for skill in speech, but in writing it can be very difficult. Many adults, as the existence of 'officialese' testifies, never really learn to do it well. Halliday's list is also valuable in pointing to the great diversity of language itself.

Professor Britton has worked from a standpoint more immediately grounded in practical English teaching, and his thinking about language relies heavily on the distinction between participants in social action and spectators of it. (See 'What's the Use' in *Language in Education*, Routledge for the Open University.) This distinction underlies the contrast between the first two of his categories of writing:

Transactional: conveying directions, asking questions, achieving day-to-day purposes, operating in society as a participant.

Expressive: exchanging feelings, airing opinions, conveying attitudes, revealing one's personality, principally though not exclusively as an observer or spectator who is not dependent on a response for the communications he makes to be valid.

Poetic: constructing (or using) a conscious artefact of language, using complex organization to grapple with complex reality.

The two accounts are not strictly comparable, since they are not analysing quite the same things. Britton focuses mainly on writing, whereas Halliday seeks to embrace spoken language as well. Moreover, Halliday is seeking to define categories which operate in any language, whether it has a literature or not, while Britton's description would seem to fit more closely the kinds of writing generated by English teaching in a culture where literature has a high place. Only a very small minority use language for poetic purposes, as Britton defines the term, but Britton and his followers make a powerful case for the educational value of setting writing tasks of a poetic nature, both in prose and verse form. It is also important to realize that both accounts are schematic: that is, no particular instance of talk will be exclusively transactional and without any expressive function at all, just as much writing by children moves uncertainly between expressive and poetic functions. In the same way, but to a much greater degree, Halliday's is an abstract account: a request to another person to shut the door is primarily regulatory in function, but if it is said and understood as a signal of intimacy between two people the interactional function is present; and if the two people are children acting out an improvisation (with a 'pretend' door), the imaginative function is being exploited as well. In fact almost any natural occurrence of language is multi-functional in this way, and Halliday intends us to see this by suggesting functions which

can all operate at the same time. It is too simple to say that Britton's
categories are mainly linguistic, but if Britton's are a useful guide in planning a programme of classwork in English, Halliday's are a useful reminder
of how much we may leave out by concentrating our work on the teaching
of writing alone.

The standing danger for non-specialists is that of asking their pupils to
write *only* expressive and poetic material, or else exclusively transactional
bread-and-butter stuff. If your taste is genuinely unsympathetic to imaginative writing, and the transactional category appeals to you, Halliday's
analysis can enable you to discriminate between representational and interactional functions, for example, which in Britton's scheme are both covered
by transactional writing. It is with older pupils, especially in further education, that writing for interactional purposes becomes important, but
success at that stage rests on experience of these functions of language in
the spoken medium much earlier in life. In any case, it may be doubted
whether children of 9 (or of 13 for that matter) are ever conscious of the
distinctions made here, or ever ought to be. The most that they normally
appreciate is that their writing will be scrutinized by the teacher; its mistakes
will be noted, sometimes annotated, and occasionally pilloried or ridiculed.
This expectation that mistakes will not be allowed to be corrected quietly
will in the end have the same effect as a foreign visitor's knowledge that his
accent is found amusing: it will dry up the flow of language altogether. We
have stressed elsewhere (see Chapter 7) that pupils' mistakes in their writing
should be noted, collected by the teacher, and dealt with in classwork or with
the individual in a fashion which does not create anxiety. The strategy of
writing very little or of saying 'Please, sir, I can't think of anything to say'
denotes the presence of anxiety or fear.

This desire to have children write more rather than less may seem
inconsistent with our earlier observation that most children are asked to
write too much in school. To be more precise, children are given too much
unmotivated writing under intense pressure of time. It is this emphasis, on
the motivation of children to write, and on the restriction of the motiveless
mechanical exercise (in English or any other subject) that underlies our
suggestions for writing work. We shall use Britton's categories rather than
Halliday's, largely for convenience, but partly because the latter were not
designed as a scheme for planning work in school.

Transactional writing

This falls into two broad categories. One is of course the wide range of
'service' functions through which a child's mastery of written language

underpins the rest of the curriculum—note-making, record-keeping, recording and giving information, writing history essays and social studies projects, writing up scientific experiments, and so on. As Douglas Barnes has pointed out, this kind of language is full of unexplored assumptions, and later in school life is liable to be a source of difficulty. (See Barnes, *Language, the Learner, and the School*, Penguin.) For example, it is readily assumed that 'dictated notes' are the same thing as 'notes', whereas in reality the operations involved are radically different. History teachers assume, for example, that after several years of having notes dictated, pupils will somehow have learned how to make their own notes on a lecture. This does not necessarily follow. The English teacher can begin, with pupils of 12, by using a tape-recorded talk on a simple subject: the class is asked to make a set of notes, to compare them in groups, decide what the main headings are, lay out a scheme, and listen to the tape again. In the same way, the ability to comprehend and later to convey instructions in writing can be put into practice in the classroom, but it is pedantic to rule out diagrams if they would be used in real life. A pupil has to give some instructions, using one of his hobbies as the subject-matter. How the group carries them out provides instant feedback, and the instructions usually have to be clarified. But it is all too easy to make the task too difficult: instructions for making a paper dart are manageable, whereas instructions for tying a tie may not be. Similar exercises can involve recipes, simple experiments, conjuring tricks, and so on, and where possible they should be based on close collaboration with specialist colleagues. How well the task of giving instructions works is determined by how well the job is done.

The second broad category of transactional writing is what one might call the social uses of language, or those parts of them which use writing. These include letters of every kind except the highly personal one (which would be under the heading of expressive writing). It is important to grasp that this category embraces writing of a wide range of formality, but that any conscious awareness of differences in formality will not develop until after the age of 13. We have suggested elsewhere a number of opportunities which arise for children to write letters, and here is a list of letters written by pairs of pupils in a class aged 10. The teacher arranged that every pupil formed one of a pair, and every pair in the class wrote one or more of the letters during the year. The total of 165 letters included the following, nearly all written on school notepaper:

Seven letters asking local officials, managers, social workers, etc., to visit the school to talk with the class.

Six letters to thank them for coming. (One refused.)

One letter to a novelist telling her how much the class had liked one of her novels.

Sixteen letters to the same novelist answering her request for much more information about what they had enjoyed in the novel.

Eight letters expressing appreciation for hospitality received during class outings and visits.

A letter to the Vicar asking him to come and show them how he did a baptism, and one to thank him for coming.

A letter to the teacher's husband to say they were sorry he had broken his arm.

Eleven letters to parents of members of the class, wives of staff, and others associated with the school, to offer congratulations on the birth of a baby.

Three letters to an L.E.A. District Inspector thanking him for arranging a special grant for a Children's Britannica.

Ten letters addressed to pupils in a special school in the district, telling them about plans for a visit by the special school's pupils to the Christmas play. In this case four of the letters were being written to immediate neighbours or siblings.

Not surprisingly, the teacher did not have to ask her class to write their thirty-four letters at the end of the year thanking her for all her hard work.

In a class where letter-writing is of this order, it becomes quite unnecessary to teach children that some letters have to be formal while some can be friendly. The layout of letters, and of the address on the envelope, becomes one of the classroom's standing displays, or is always available on a reference sheet.

Another common activity in this category arises from meetings. Even in junior school the pupils should be consulted about some aspects of school life, and every time this happens is a chance to ask some pupil to practise the demanding art of taking minutes. A class newspaper provides many opportunities for factual reporting, and the many outside contacts which we have suggested provide other occasions for simple transactional uses of language

To sum up, we can suggest that each pupil should in the course of a term's work gain experience, of a kind appropriate to his own attainment, of using writing for requests, replies, reports, recording, describing, and handling impressions and ideas. A great deal of this work will occur naturally in the course of pursuing other studies, and many English teachers have sought to use their own work on written language almost exclusively for the last of our list. It is this sense of needing to plug a gap in the rest of the curriculum which probably accounts for the tenacity of the long outmoded form known as 'essay'. However, most of the children under 13 are still in the phase of what Piaget called concrete operations: they do not handle abstractions or generalized concepts easily. There should be no place whatever, therefore, for writing tasks which depend on one-word titles, or call for assessment of long-term changes, or ask for speculations. If speculation has a place in the writing of children of this age, as it clearly should, it will be in the form of imaginative prediction, and hence in the category of expressive writing.

Our use of the distinction between transactional and expressive should not be taken to imply that the former is solely nuts-and-bolts, bread-and-butter stuff with no use for imagination or insight. Transactions are, by definition, social activities which engage with other persons. Children need to learn some of the elements of varying what they write to match the person to whom it is being addressed. In the middle school range this control will develop in spoken language first, and only to a rudimentary degree in writing. But the response of the recipient of a letter can and should be explored in drama, and the various possible ways of wording letters of, for instance, complaint, can be investigated. Teachers who have not related written work to drama before will be surprised by the effect of doing this: it reveals vividly the concreteness Piaget refers to. By contrast, the kind of language sought by many secondary teachers of history, for example, entails the accurate handling of impersonal and passive constructions which are markedly abstract, and a type of transactional writing for which most pupils under 13 are not yet ready.

Expressive writing
We have largely avoided the term 'creative' writing, if only because all children's writing must be derivative to greater or lesser degree. In recent years many English teachers have fallen into the error of supposing that this is the only kind of writing worth doing in English lessons. Indeed, at all levels expressive writing has an important part to play. It can also lead to work of outstanding merit, as Sir Alec Clegg's anthology *The Excitement of Writing* (Chatto and Windus) well shows. But teachers have encountered the uncomfortable fact that not all children readily demonstrate what this

approach would call imagination. Partly in consequence of this, whole theories
of English teaching and whole course books have been based on the notion of
'English through experience'—the theory that children should be encouraged
to observe accurately and then write powerfully and expressively about their
experience. But 'observe accurately' can very easily slip into 'feel acutely'
and even 'suffer painfully'. Thus, boys and girls have often been sent to
run round a snow-covered field in winter in order to 'have something to
write about' afterwards. A.W. Rowe and P. Emmens' course books,
English Through Experience (Blond Educational), dating from the mid-
sixties, actually suggest that pupils prick their fingers with a pin: 'the
sharp sting of the pain is a powerful stimulus'. There is a paradox, somewhere, in basing imaginative writing on something so unimaginary, not
to say unimaginative, as a pin-prick. But the real objection to this sort of
approach is that it can limit the imagination rather than extend it, while
extending imaginative experience can be done very well by vicarious and
artistic means.

Expressive writing does usually need a stimulus of some kind. This should
usually be something worth a child's attention in its own right, and we have
seen very successful work based on slides, photographs, and reproductions
of great painting. Non-naturalistic art has often proved good material, as
have the Impressionist painters. Slides are better suited to group work, and
reproductions to work of detail. (Full details of sources for this kind of
material are given in Sources and Resources I.) Film-loops are also useful,
especially the Nuffield science ones of a chicken emerging from its egg, and
of a factory chimney being demolished. (The latter also shows the process
in reverse.) On a larger scale, films can be one of the most useful of all
stimuli to expressive writing. Music is useful, too, whether for the purpose of
creating a 'mood', or as folk song for participation, and there is a useful list
of the former in R.M. Pemberton-Billing and J. Clegg's *Teaching Drama*
(University of London Press), pp.140—44. There is also much useful
guidance in T.G. Jeremiah's *Source Book of Creative Themes* (Blackwell).

Most of the writing produced in response to stimuli like these will
consist of short pieces. There is also a need for practice in more extended
expressive writing. For the more able child it is far from unthinkable to
suggest writing a novel. Many others can be encouraged to keep a personal
journal. In this, children are encouraged to write about their own feelings,
hopes, fears, activities, and friends, on the basis that there will be no
marking or correcting. The value of this lies in its encouragement of fluency
and organizing private experience into a semi-public statement; it has been
found particularly successful with less able pupils. (For an outstanding

example, see Dan Fader, *Hooked on Books*, Pergamon.) Expressive writing
generally, of course, calls for a lighter hand in the marking than does transactional or poetic writing, which can be tested against the response of a
likely audience. The lesser formality and the more personal nature of
expressive writing make it important in the period when children are beginning to discover and explore their own identities. What expressive writing
should not do is monopolize the children's written work.

Poetic writing

The conscious shaping and ordering of experience and feeling may relate
to real or imaginary worlds, and must be expected to develop relatively late
in the 9 to 13 age range, if at all. It will find its place in two main areas, of
which the first is naturally the writing of fiction. Short stories use a
sophisticated literary form, and children of this age should not be expected
to write them very often. When they do, they should be held to a limited
length, and it is a very useful maxim to suggest that pupils try to tell us as
much as possible about as few characters and events as possible. These
ground-rules are not restrictive so much as supportive: they prevent the
pupil from rambling and they focus his attention on the essential point of
the activity. As we have said, the novel, which can be better described to
pupils as a long story, is a possible form, and there are several well-worn
but useful literary models—the shipwreck, the dangerous journey, the alien
visitor, the family that lost its parents, being caught by pirates, to name
but a few which have served both distinguished writers and young appren-
tices well. With pupils of 10 or 11, it is wise to sketch out a structure. With
'Shipwreck', for example, the chapters might be:

1. The shipwreck
2. I reach an island
3. I explore the island
4. The island is inhabited
5. Meeting with a stranger
6. Escape

Children naturally hanker after illustrating their writing, and with some
children the amount of writing they can do will be limited to making the
captions for their pictures, but the skills of construction and organization
cannot be learned in the abstract.

The second main sphere for poetic writing is of course verse. There are
still a few schools where children under 11 encounter no poetry other than
ballads and hymns. It is not surprising that such pupils know of no verse

which does not limit itself to loud rhymes and sprung rhythm. This leads
to an obtrusive reliance on rhyme as a defining feature of 'poetry'. Only a
few poets in this century have relied heavily on rhyme, and they with
subtlety (see the work of Wilfred Owen and R.S. Thomas). If children
of 9 have not met poetry which offers more than regular metre and strong
rhyme, it is time they did, although poetry anthologies seem to be the
most enduring and least renewable of school textbooks. The aim here
must be to enable children to experience a way of writing which is com-
pressed, perhaps oblique or elliptical, impressionistic and unelaborate. Only
when children have grasped that this is not in any sense an odd way of
writing should they be encouraged to write in the same way. The best term
to use is free verse. Basically, each new thought emerges as a separate line;
speech rhythms reinforce the meaning; and the line is as long as it needs
to be. Here are two examples, by pupils of 11.

Looking out of the Window at Night

I can see myself;
If I look more closely,
I can see outside in the street.
It is hard to see it all clearly.
The privet hedges are glistening with the raindrops.
The window pane is blurred with the rain.
The lawn has got little lights on, of raindrops.
It is like being in a fishtank
Looking at the world.
I can see the rain
Bounding off the pavement.
Great puddles of water.
The privet shivers.

The Graveyard

The short cut
Over bushes and nettles
Into the graveyard.
Large white tombstones, In Memory Of . . . .
Here Lies . . . .
To some people they bring back memories,
Ghostly memories.

Both of these are typical of the writing of children of this age. They demonstrate a movement from expressive to poetic writing, with an attempt at
conscious shaping of experience presented by a first-hand impression. The

absorption in the facts being seen is striking. By the age of 13 one of the
writers was producing this poem, after seeing a slide of a detail of the
Creation of Adam in the Sistine Chapel:

The Creation

Creation made me,
I am man;
Creation breathed in me,
I am man;
Creation moved me,
I am man;
Creation loves me,
I am man.

Children who can develop writing of this kind acquire another means of
exploring and coming to terms with experience. For many of them the
compression of statement and the freedom to be inexplicit offer a most
valuable way of learning to control language, one result of which may
be a much increased power over prose writing. But this is not perhaps the
main value of free verse. Some children have been found to become articulate in writing in no other form. Here is an example of a boy of 14, writing
about a cock-fight and its consequences:

Blind John

Big blind John he comes from West Brom
He went to Bidul stone fair to buy some
ribbion for his wifes hair

her hair was gold her dress was
green but by him unseen

He wasn't a betting man until he got to
the fair, When he heard of a cockfight
going on there he could not see but he
went all the same,
The owners didn't bother to them it was a
game.

Then John looked at the money and looked
yet in his mind he new what was right
John was all big and strong yet he new
It was wrong to bet on the old and not on the young
The old uns blood was split all over the
sand now the proud owner held out
his hand.

now the old had lost so had John
now all the money was gone. now no
ribbion for his wifes hair so it would
have to stay bare.

When he got hom he was happy and
gay, but his bad news was goin to
end a bieutiful day.
he said to his wife in a slow and low voice
dear I am sorry theres no ribbion for your
hair cos I spent the money on bidleston
fair.

This poem is interesting for a number of reasons. There are clear signs that
the boy who wrote it is still in the grip of assumptions that poetry should
rhyme. As he becomes more engaged by writing it, his rhythmical control
becomes much more marked, and the writing gains force and economy.
The initial inspiration for this poem, too, clearly grew out of poetry that
had been read aloud and talked about. This background includes 'Wednesbury
Cocking' (in Robert Graves, *English and Scottish Ballads*, Heinemann), and
D.H. Lawrence's short story 'Strike Pay' (in *Collected Short Stories*,
Heinemann). The piece is a good illustration of how poetic writing may well
be the most appropriate and mature response that children of this age can
make to literature. (We have printed this piece uncorrected. Generally,
however, we believe that children's writing should be published very
sparingly, and should normally be printed in conventional spelling which
the writer has taken part in securing. There is reason to think that the vogue
for printing uncorrected texts of children's writing may have led to an
over indulgence of lazy writing.)

    There are other poetic forms available, of course, beside the free verse
one. The 'haiku' and 'shape poems' are useful exercises, and there are many
examples for study and exercises for use in Books I and II of *Touchstones*
(University of London Press), a 'teaching anthology of poetry' by
M.G. and P. Benton. This is more valuable with children of 11 to 13. For
younger children there is a very useful collection in *Happenings* I (Harrap),
by M. Wollman and D. Grugeon, and we list other anthologies in Sources
and Resources I. To avoid misunderstanding, before leaving the subject of
poetic writing, let us add that we regard the study of poetry as a study of
ways of writing and an avenue into new interpretations of experience. To
use poetry for rote-learning adds nothing to the competence of the child
as a user of language and devalues the poetry he learns.

    Finally, it is implicit in all we have said about poetic writing that it may

take the form of prose as well as verse, and that some pupils find prose
the easier form. There is a fine account of children learning to write in
poetic modes by J.W.P. Creber in his *Sense and Sensitivity* (University of
London Press), which also offers the teacher a great deal of help with
leading children into such work. However, one impression which the non-
specialist may derive from such a book is that pupils should spend a high
proportion of their time writing. We believe that schoolchildren spend too
much time writing already, and the emphasis we have placed on other
activities—listening, talking, and reading—is designed to foster an English
curriculum in which they write better, partly because they write less.

Standards

Much that we have said in these pages could be represented as disregarding
standards of excellence. This would be a serious misunderstanding. We have
stressed the difference between spoken and written language because we
believe that teachers who possess this understanding will enable more of
their pupils, in the long run, to become better writers. We have advocated
more, and more sustained, exposure to good literature and good writing in
the 9 to 13 age range, because we believe that children who do not read
enough, in quantity or quality, will not write as well as they would otherwise.
But to emphasize, as we must, the length and difficulty of a journey which
a pupil must travel before he becomes a skilled writer is not at all to decry
the value or the importance of the journey itself.

   There are children—a few—who by the age of 13 will be mature and
practised writers. Pupils who can attain this mastery can also sustain the
full rigour of our critical inspection, and one of the dangers of mixed-
ability teaching is that they may escape our attention. But the broad run
of children are helped along the road by support and encouragement rather
than by severe critiques. And while some children of 13 can and do read
Dickens for enjoyment, they will also from time to time read
John Wyndham or Ian Fleming or Dennis Wheatley as do many who
teach them. Even the most able pupil, however, is unlikely to want to
write like these novelists, and he should certainly not be expected to.
Children should be expected to write like themselves—and to do it
to the top of their bent. It is fallacious to equate the standards of
a school's English teaching with the repute of the authors studied. There
is no educational merit in expecting children of 13, however intelligent,
to understand the subtleties of mature Shakespearean tragedy or the
racked density of Donne.

There is a much more genuine problem in assessing the writing of the
most successful pupils in the middle school range. The very best of such
work will often be close to meriting publication, but it is by its very nature
private work, written as a rule for the eye of the teacher alone. Moreover
it will often be astonishingly diverse: the good English teacher will be
receiving sets of work from a class of 13 year olds, which include short
stories, poems, impressions, tirades, comments, and so forth, and much of
it so consistently good as to defy conventional grading or marking. Maintaining what are glibly called 'standards' in such a situation can often be
much harder work than with more average performers. One piece may
remind the teacher of a poem by a major author; it should be looked up,
and the reference given in the comment. Another may be a bitter account
of a W.I. meeting, and the teacher may want the child to look at similar
passages by Charlotte Brontë or Trollope—more digging. A third piece
prompts a look at the ethologists such as Lorenz or Tinbergen. This kind
of response is what the work of the ablest pupils often deserves but rarely
receives, because it is hard work and calls for very well-read teachers. Both
the authors have done this work for long enough to know that it is facile
to identify all grammar school English teaching as traditional. Likewise, the
problem of maintaining standards, or securing the very best attainments
that one's pupils can achieve, is not solved simply by collecting the ablest
children together in special schools or streams. Indeed, the whole point
about standards is that they need mediating to far more pupils than a
selective system can ever touch.

There is related problem for school librarians. While they are professionally
right in refusing to spend public money on stocking up with Dennis Wheatley
or Hank Jansen, there is a distinction between the standards they promulgate
as librarians and the range of reading which pupils can usefully engage in.
Because a school will not supply certain kinds of reading does not imply
that children should never read them. To confuse the professional duty of
the librarian in a school with the moral welfare of the pupils is easily done
but mistaken. Such a confusion will ultimately weaken the credibility of
the school's values in the eyes of the children: a school library *has* to exercise
some limited kinds of censorship, but it should be one based on literary
merit, not on an anxious desire to avoid upsetting parents or ill-informed
laymen.

The standards involved in English teaching, finally, are those of the
English teacher and his professional colleagues, not those of teachers or
parents who think, because they are speakers of English, that they are
thereby qualified to say what its teaching should be about.

Chapter 7

Survival – marking and assessment

'Survival' may seem a melodramatic title for this chapter—until you have tried to sustain the full burden of a normal teaching week for a whole school year with several classes of a wide range of ability. We are concerned here not so much with discipline as with fatigue: English teaching can be desperately hard work. We have stressed that good work in English springs from relationships of trust and respect between teachers and pupils. This means that some of the disciplinary measures available to schools are not usable by the English teacher: no child can come to trust a teacher who is liable to twist his ear or storm with unpredictable anger. But, at the same time, no child can respect a teacher personally if he cannot first respect him for his basic class-control. Moreover, talk-laden group work in English makes special demands on the teacher, and if he is trying to encourage talk he has to be very sparing in his use of the traditional classroom command to 'Shut up!' For all these reasons, it is a rare English specialist who has not experienced quite serious fatigue at some stage early in his career. The non-specialist, rightly giving his attention to his main field of interest, is likely to feel his stint of English teaching demanding to a disproportionate degree. One of the messages of this book to secondary head teachers, therefore, is that English is a subject which should be distributed to non-specialist teachers less freely than it often has been. The main purpose of this chapter, however, is to outline some ways of keeping the work-load of English teaching within reasonable bounds.

Marking

In a nutshell, many teachers of English adopt the policy of 'get them working and keep up with it if you can', whereas they ought to adopt the policy of 'arrange the work so that you *can* keep up with it'. In this way of putting it, 'keep up with' is apt to be thought of as meaning, simply, 'marking'. For teachers of some subjects, this may be the case. But in English the work often relates to feelings as well as to ideas, and hence may call for *response* rather than marking. What are marks in a pupil's book if not messages from teacher to pupil? The simplest message of all may well be a bare tick: it says, 'You have done your bit, and I have taken notice.' Even this basic message is worth conveying: the class whose books are never marked very soon learns that its teacher is not interested in what his pupils are doing. In this sense, all marking is a form of response. Conventional practice in the past has conflated this simple message of response with another one, of evaluation—'. . .and this is how well you have done it.' Often in the work of an English teacher a tick or a brief comment will be *better* than a numerical mark, and a comment which gives a reason or points to a better way of doing it will be better still. If this seems an impossible standard to maintain, as it is for teachers whose pupils write something every week, the only recourse is to be selective. That is, some pupils' work will receive a tick or two at one marking and a fuller comment at the next, and the pupils have in effect to take their turn for the teacher's close attention but are never wholly neglected.

The teacher requiring a steady flow of marks to accumulate in his book may look on this view of marking in English with dismay. But learning vocabularies for French or formulae for chemistry is only one kind of learning, and, in developing competence in the native language, not the most helpful one. The school system as a whole places much reliance on the use of 'learning homework' and 'exercises' which produce work that can be given a score. The pupils who undergo an education heavily focused on scoring numerical marks in tests are being given a powerful message that marks are one of the main things that schooling is all about. In English work there is a place for the exercise which can be given a score, but it is a very limited place. Tests and exercises designed to produce scores to be entered in the mark-book are usually selected so as to yield a range of marks which lead to a rank-order within a class. Such a pattern places some pupils at the bottom end of the order and the implication is that this will stimulate them to further effort. In the experience of all too many teachers this simply does not work in English: rather, low marks tend to demoralize and discoura There is a difference, that is, between having high standards and being ungen- erous with one's marks or grades. But there is a deeper reason for not using easily-marked tests and exercises in the routine of English teaching: compete in using language cannot be measured on numerical scales. All that can be measured in any one instance is the pupil's ability to use language in a particu lar context for a particular purpose. This was underlined by Dr. H. Rosen's research at the London Institute of Education, which revealed that a candidate's grade in O-Level English could well depend, as much as on any other factor, on what *kind* of topic he chose in the essay paper. (This work is in Rosen's unpublished London University Ph.D. thesis. For a summary, see J. Pearce, *Examinations in English*, Papers in Linguistics and English Teaching, Series II, Longman.)

In practice, however, many teachers have to work within a system that relies heavily on marks as the main incentive for the pupil. If you are teaching English in such a school, you will feel compelled, perhaps reluctantly, to go along with the system. But accepting this constraint does not mean that the English teacher should apply it to everything that his pupils do, not only because it would then be impossible to keep up with the work. The real task that is being done when an English teacher is marking written work is mainly one of responding, and should be only in very small degree one of assessing. Even here, the assessing should be designed to monitor the pupil's progress. Better than a formal examination, the regular written work of a class can tell the teacher what changes in their language competence are occurring (or not occurring). This is essential feed-back to the teacher about his own successes and failures. The improvements he has sought through his own planning of activities and instruction need to be watched for. But, although these objectives may be clear in the teacher's mind, achieving them is likely to be a slow process. For example, exercises about where to put in commas and full stops in a passage printed without any in a textbook may yield an easy set of marks out of ten, but there is little or no evidence that the pupils show any benefit from the exercise in their own writing. This means that the slowness with which language competence develops can be disheartening to the pupil as well as to the teacher, and the pupils need constant reassurance that they are not wasting their efforts. Similarly, high marks in exercises, which are no necessary sign of competence in our sense, may also mislead pupils.

The English teacher who systematically encourages his pupil is not betraying any standards: he is maintaining and building the relationships on which good work in English has to be based. The encouragement needs to be related, not to the work of other pupils, but to the earlier work of the same pupil. Many classes in the 9 to 13 age range are of mixed ability and the pupils are vividly conscious of the differences among themselves. If a child has invested a great deal of effort and commitment in a piece of writing which, *for him*, is a remarkable advance, it should be treated as such. Merely to dismiss it as nothing like as good as the achievements of the more able children in the class will only damage the child and weaken his developing sense of his own identity. The encouraging comment, sincerely meant, however brief, is the English teacher's most powerful weapon. It is utterly at variance with this to adopt what Andrew Wilkinson has nicely described as the role of 'the teacher as self-appointed proof-reader . . . GRowling and SPitting and hiSSing from the margin . . .' Many non-specialist teachers of English have never encountered any other way of doing 'marking', and have forgotten that children only learn from marginal annotations like *Gr, Sp., P, Slang, Para*, if they are made to. Psychologically, too, the liberal use of red ink gives a visual and mental prominence to mistakes, and can have the effect of actually ingraining them more deeply than before, especially with spelling.

If the teacher is going to invest the time needed for close marking of a set of compositions, he ought to extract some return on his investment. Some teachers do this by using a simple dot or a question-mark, leaving each pupil to work out precisely what is wrong and put it right at each point. Some set the class up in groups of four or five, and ask each group to read all the compositions written by the group; each group spends some time discussing the items pointed out by the close marking (and any others the members of the group may notice), rough notes are made, and the pupils re-write. Meanwhile the teacher has moved from group to group, listening hard (which can be a vividly instructive experience), and intervening only at key points. In the junior school class, this activity may be used for most of the class, while the teacher deals with a small group whose written work has been very limited. In many cases the children will want to write in collaboration, and this should be encouraged too. But in all these cases the close marking has preceded and formed the basis for further class activity, as it should.

Classes whose writing is sometimes marked in detail and sometimes marked only by impression may lead parents or colleagues to ask why so many 'obvious errors' and 'glaring blunders' are allowed to pass un-noticed. The teacher's reply can be forthright and easily understood: some work is marked closely, some is impression-marked, and some is personal expressive writing which is not meant for marking at all. In other words, the teacher knows what he is doing and can describe his policy. But there is a deeper issue here. The English teacher's job is to foster each individual's linguistic growth. There will inevitably be cases where a child who is regularly making a particular mistake needs to be allowed to go on making it, because he is not yet ready to learn otherwise. For example, a child of 9 who is only just mastering continuous reading is likely to be very uncertain about some of his letters in his writing. The teacher might be wise to hold off any pressure to get all the written forms right until the child has had a much longer exposure to written text in his reading. Again, few children of 14 can handle the syntax of impersonal constructions, chiefly because impersonal forms are very rare in spoken language. Hence, they may begin with 'One might think . . .' and quickly lapse into the second person. Again, many adults believe that the first or second person form of address is a defect in written English, but if you have read our earlier chapters carefully you will have met many instances of this, and scarcely have noticed them. One of the English teacher's headaches is the liberal supply of advice from colleagues who claim to know what English is, and it is usually better to suffer it in silence. Secondary head-teachers who lack specialist competence should be particularly guarded in their definitions of objectives in English.

Constructive marking

There are four kinds of outcome of pupils' 'work' which the English teacher can plan for, and they demand different amounts of his time for marking or responding. The first category is the kind of work which can be handled very quickly with the whole class—the spelling test, the course-book exercise, and the word game. If these are used as mark-book fodder, totals in the mark-book are not likely to represent the real merits of the pupils' work. As we have seen, not all such exercises are productive. If they deal exclusively with spelling, or punctuation, they are also conveying to a class that the teacher thinks these things matter—as they do. But if they deal with minutiae which current usage is rapidly giving up, like the apostrophe or the distinction between single quotes and double quotes, they are not really helping the pupils, and will confuse most children under 13 anyway.

The second category of output is oral or dramatic work which calls for nothing more than the approving remark or the searching question that signals the teacher's concern. Because dramatic work does not get 'marked' does not mean it is less important. One aspect of the teacher's job here is to notice which pupils are inarticulate or reluctant talkers, and to devise situations where such pupils can begin to talk more freely. The role of talk in the growth of language competence is a subtle one, and much harm has been done by the misconception that 'Oral English' is a different kind·of English from 'ordinary' English. As we stress in Chapter 4, the less out-of-the-ordinary the role of talk can be made in English work, and the less like formal speech-making it becomes, the more productive it will be for the pupil. This must mean that marking oral work is better not attempted at all.

The third category of output is written work in a draft form, while the fourth is written work in a finished form. Writing which is in a tentative or draft stage is much more important in real life than practice in English teaching allows for. Most adults, faced with a delicate situation in which a

letter has to be written, will make one or two attempts at drafting it before
settling on a version which is fit to send. In business or academic life, too,
very few documents of any significance achieve their final form at first
drafting. The history of literature is full of instances of the endless toil of
constant re-writing, from Spenser to Richard Hughes. The school-age pupil
who can perform like a Dickens, writing out his precisely calculated thirty-
two page episodes of great and intricately planned novels with scarcely a
preliminary sketch, simply does not exist. The ability to produce finished
text at first writing is, indeed, the defining feature of the journalist, who
does not rank very highly as a literary artist in most minds. What does
exist is a strange belief that what a pupil writes down is of virgin status, not
to be deflowered by amendment or improvement. Most laymen and many
teachers seem to think in the same way—that what the children have
written is fixed, unalterable because it is in black and white, incapable of
benefit from critical comment or constructive discussion. 'Don't cross out'
is a profoundly damaging rule to impose on schoolchildren.

The only lasting way of conveying the lesson that language does not
necessarily come naturally off the top of one's head is by the use of group
work. For example, four or five boys aged 11 can take their several attempts
to describe in precise detail what it felt like to get up and go to school after
a week off with 'flu. They can read each other's efforts, and learn first that
incautious comment may expose them to ripostes about their own writing
which can hurt. This basically social discipline is also a linguistic one, of
learning to verbalize their ideas about how things can be said and written.
They go on to talk to one another about their pieces; they borrow and
plagiarize, delete this and give more weight to that; they may talk in pairs
at first and only develop a group pattern slowly. As this develops, the teache
directs attention more precisely to more particular aspects of what has been
written. The pieces which began as individual drafts may come out as four
or five pieces revised by the group and re-written by the individuals, or the
five originals may emerge as a single, collaborative piece of writing: much
depends on the age and maturity of the children. The later development may
lead groups to be set particular tasks, but the concrete task can also be used
as a way of starting a group off.

For example, one of the authors visited a school in the course of his
duties, and at the teacher's request read the end-of-the-day story to the top
class in a small rural school where the pupils ranged from 8 to 11. Next
morning the teacher asked the top juniors, ten children aged 10 and 11, to
work in two groups on as accurate and detailed a description as possible of
the man who had read to them the previous day. They took a very long time

to agree on the facts. The teacher left them to write in twos, and they pooled their efforts later, but the writing was not particularly out of the ordinary. However, a week later the visitor returned to the class, and was subjected to intense scrutiny, and to a string of questions about the right words to describe almost everything in his appearance and dress. Having to record their impressions had led the children to a much greater attentiveness to what they saw. Having seen with this new awareness they were then able to record what they saw with striking accuracy.

Further up the age range, the kinds of writing which children can be asked to undertake naturally become more differentiated. Some tasks will be (to use Britton's terms) transactional, some expressive, some poetic. By this stage, however, the children should ideally have become so used to group work on their writing, and so accustomed to the value of sub-editing, that the restraint which many teachers feel about applying this to expressive writing disappears. More significant still, children will enter the 14+ stage, where English specialists are constantly urging them to plan what they write and to review what they have written, already taking it for granted that finished writing needs to be finished. Whether they continue to need editing sessions for this, or undertake it in pairs or on their own, will be for the teacher to judge.

Where and how the teacher makes his assessments in this cycle of talking and drafting and editing and finishing will have to depend on the nature of the task. But the teacher is not simply there to act as Feared Examiner at the end: he is there as the one adult speaker and writer in the room, and, one hopes, as a trusted supporter who can supply advice, fact, guidance, and the security (which some children may always need) of saying No. Most teachers will want to 'do their marking' on the finished work. If the work is the product of two or three pupils, it is no less capable of being marked because of that. Some teachers will see their role, in respect of maintaining standards, as better fulfilled by going round the room while the groups are at work, alerting the groups to matters which will not satisfy him, guiding them away from unforeseen difficulties, encouraging tentative experiment, and above all, when work is produced which gives pleasure, allowing his pupils to see and recognize his joy. A girl of 14 in a mixed grammar school was describing her English teacher to her parents: 'Do him a good essay and he's like a little boy with a bag of sweets.' Exactly.

If the teacher can discriminate between the four categories of output—the snap test, oral and dramatic work, draft writing, and finished writing—he can control how he distributes his available time for marking. This control takes time to acquire, just as the skills of preparation described in other

chapters do. So most teachers of English have at some time to admit
momentary defeat. There is no loss of face in saying to a class 'I am sorry,
but there just has not been time to mark your stories. Get into groups of
five, work out which is the best story in your group, and appoint someone
to read it out.' If English teaching includes moral honesty and integrity
among its values, English teachers may sometimes have to show those
values in practice, and their pupils will respect them for it.

Throughout his work, the English teacher is watching and listening for
information about how his pupils are progressing, looking for what needs
doing next, and planning how to do it. This monitoring is possibly the most
difficult part of it all, because it entails a process of looking beneath the
surface of the language the children use and sensing what language they
need to learn how to use.

In fact, much of the language that comes through on paper is the child's
native spoken language. This language is not defective or incorrect as such.
For many children, *not* to say 'we was' or 'he done' would be to mark
themselves off socially and invite rejection or ridicule from their peers. If
the teacher seeks to displace this native speech with what he or the school
regards as a better one, he is bound to fail. Our only hope of success lies in
helping pupils to learn more than one way of wording their messages. (Lots
of educated people can talk plain if they want, though they don't often do
it 'cos they think it's beneath 'em.) To put this technically, people need a
repertoire of ways of speaking. A first step, therefore, must be to familiarize
the children with the way of writing which is customary in most written
English, suggesting to them not that this is how they should talk but that
this is another possible way of talking and writing *in addition* to their own.
Many children begin to acquire a repertoire of ways of speaking by mimicry
and through drama work. Others feel their way into it by reading aloud.

In monitoring his pupils' work, the English teacher needs to select and
order his priorities. With classes whose written English is thoroughly bad, he
is rather in the position of the good disciplinarian teaching in a school where
everybody else is lax: he cannot solve the problem on his own. There are
some classes, especially where first-year secondary groups have been rigidly
streamed, which seem to offer no hope of improvement. The priorities in
such cases include, high on the list, a policy of putting right the errors of
previous teaching, especially that of *expecting children to write before they
have become reasonably experienced readers*. It would be a bold specialist
who scrapped all sustained writing in the English work of such a class, and
did as much reading as possible for three months, but at least this would
have the priorities the right way round. (One of us once did just this with

a fifth form!) Written language cannot be learned from a spoken language environment: it can only be learned from written language. One element in the teacher's survival, that is to say, is a realistic assessment of what he can hope to achieve with a class in the time he has available.

But in the best of all worlds, emergencies can still occur: lesson material goes astray, colleagues fall ill, a well-planned sequence of work ends two periods earlier than expected, or the bell goes and a homework has to be set in a hurry. In this last case it is better not to set it: unplanned homework is a menace. The basic strategy here is to ensure that each pupil is equipped with a book which he is currently reading. For classwork, the real danger is the 'discussion lesson'. Many a teacher, at the end of a tiring day, lost for an idea with 2B, has fallen for this temptation. The truth of the matter is that if a discussion lesson is to engage the pupils for more than 10% of the talk, the teacher is going to be working at maximum concentration. If the teacher is exhausted, the class will sit back and play the game of 'Get Teacher Talking'.

So every English teacher needs a bank or store of constructive materials for use in near-emergency situations, which make the pupils do the work and set the teacher free to move about the room, talk quietly with individuals, get the mark-book up-to-date, or to see a visiting parent while a colleague sits in. If the school or department issues a course book, it will usually have a number of pieces of lesson-fodder of this sort—but it takes experience and luck to use this source without having combed through it beforehand. As a resource for dealing with emergencies, however, such as an absent colleague, M. Gatter and N. Kelly's *Photocards for English* (Edward Arnold) are particularly good, and the teacher's book is helpful. Peter Abbs' *English Broadsheets* (Heinemann) also provide material of this kind. With much more flexibility than a course book or exercise allows, especially for mixed-ability classes, these materials are nevertheless no substitutes for properly planned English work.

Examinations

Each category of output calls for a different kind of response or 'marking' from the teacher. The drift of our analysis is towards reducing the burden of conventional 'marking' that falls on the teacher of English. In other chapters we have suggested that English is largely an individual pursuit. The combined effect of these two parts of our argument could well seem an

opposition to all formal assessment and examining in English. In an ideal
world this would indeed be the case, but a particular subject will claim
immunity from assessment only at the cost of a lot of its prestige. From
the school's point of view, there are bound to be examinations in English
at some stage before the children are 13. English departments have to
devise ways of limiting the harm that examinations can do to English
teaching and language learning.

The literature about the bad influence of examinations on English was
referred to in Chapter 1. Its argument is that language is complex and its
uses are many and various, while examinations have to be simple and their
samplings arbitrary. Further, some types of question used in English
examinations have had a widespread and very harmful influence on
classroom teaching. More technically, a single sample of children's work at
a particular time cannot measure the growth of competence properly.
Growth in language competence is growth, not a track-race. What the
English teacher needs is not scores and exam results, but informative
records and periodic notes about individuals. But the school needs examination results. Can English departments provide these without doing too
much violence to their proper professional aims? In our view this is quite
feasible by the use of a 'profile' which evaluates all aspects of a pupil's
attainment continuously, rather than relying on final or annual written
tests.

In junior schools where 11+ selection has ceased, formal examinations
are rare, although some standardized tests may be applied. This absence of
examinations makes it peculiarly important for teachers of third and fourth-
year junior classes to compare their pupils' work and to assess it. In larger
junior schools there is a need for a senior member of the staff to act as
co-ordinator and guide, but this need is much more commonly recognized
in mathematics than in English. Continuous assessment is a vogue label for
what many teachers of upper juniors do all the time, but this does not tell
the teacher what precisely is being assessed. For a child of 10, the following
questions amount to a practicable indication of reasonable attainment:

a) Can he engage in conversation with his peers or with sympathetic
    adults in order to provide and obtain information, to convey messages
    or instructions, to describe his needs, to express his wishes, hopes, and
    anxieties, and to give imaginative expression to his inner feelings?
b) Can he use written language for a similar range of purposes, but to a
    less finished degree which is adequate for his needs as a learner?
c) Can he read a continuous story appropriate to his age and interests
    with pleasure, and can he use source books and reference materials to
    obtain information he needs?

Generalizations are dangerous, but in most of the junior school classes which the authors have observed, the majority of children would meet the third of these criteria rather more successfully than the others, and the first area appears to fall a long way behind the second. We regard this lack of oral competence as serious.

In any school where formal examinations are required, the English department should seek for the arrangement now widespread in C.S.E. and O-Level, whereby up to half of the marks are awarded by the class teacher on the basis of work done during the period under review. The written examination can then be confined to a single test. (Oral testing is laborious, unreliable, and distorts the preparatory work, often seriously.) What is known about the span of concentration of most children under 13 suggests that a written examination should ideally last no more than an hour. Also there should not be more than two of them in a day. Separate tests in language and literature at this level lead to testing the pupils' memory of books they have read. This is utterly deplorable, since the books ought to be read for pleasure rather than to be grindingly committed to memory. The separation also leads to language tests which assess what children know *about* language, not how well they can *use* it. Nor should there be the uneasy compromise of setting comprehension passages out of classic novels, which are too difficult for most children anyway. Separating language and literature is a layman's notion of English which specialists have been seeking to escape from.

If pupils of 11 or 12 must do an English examination, let them be given an informative piece of prose to read and some tasks which cannot be carried out if they have not understood it; or alternatively be given an object that leads to a specific writing task. For example, a factual description of a house can lead to the task of sketching the plan; a colour photograph of a family can lead to the task of describing them for a stranger. Such a task should occupy a third of the hour. During the rest of the time, the pupil should be invited to write on one, or with less able pupils, two from a list of topics. The way these topics are formulated is important. Here are two English examinations set in 1972 to first-year pupils in large comprehensive schools:

A. 1. Horses. (Do *not* tell a story.)
   2. Is it becoming too dangerous to cycle on our roads?
   3. Describe in detail the happiest day of your last holidays.
   4. The house you would like when you are grown up.
B. 1. On the back wall of the room are six pictures. If you wish, go and study them, select *one*, and write about the feelings it stirs up in your mind. (Poems are allowed.)

2. Tell a story about a pet which goes lame, with or without a happy ending.
3. Imagine the ideal day in your next school holidays, suppose it has already happened, and describe the important parts of it.
4. Choose one of the Shelter posters on the wall facing you, imagine yourself as one of the people in it, and write about a day or an event which fits that person.

The first set is of course sterile, mainly through failure to predict the inevitable results. Girls of 12, asked to write about horses, want to tell a story— why go out of the way to frustrate them? How can a 12 year old assess the trend factor in 'Is it becoming . . .'? The third topic invites vagueness, so far in the past is the event. The teacher who set the second group had grasped the value of stimulus, and naturally he received imaginative writing. His pupils were used to the distractions of several stimuli, and knew how to select. Their answers were roughly four times as long as those of the pupils of very similar ability who faced the first set.

What are we assessing?

At the upper end of the age range we are discussing, the linguistic demands of the rest of the curriculum become much more severe. As it is taught further up the school, each subject calls increasingly upon its own technical vocabulary, and perhaps also on the grammatical features which are typical of it. To some extent it is natural for teachers to look for analogous developments in the writing of their pupils. In particular, they come to place a premium on explicitness: usage such as 'you know' and 'sort of', words which are vague rather than specific, and elliptical phrasing need to be outgrown. This set of features of writing which is thought of as immature is very closely associated, however, with grammatical or syntactic patterns. Explicit and accurate expression calls for considerable skill with such key patterns as the noun phrase: for example, in scientific prose. Much the same considerations apply to the pupil's ability to handle the tense system of written English, and to make use of its many kinds of qualifying clause. Another way in which teachers more or less unconsciously expect their pupils' writing to mature is in the smoothness with which the sentences are made to hang together and 'flow'. These attributes of good writing are as characteristic of imaginative writing as they are of transactional writing, and it is possible to develop formal criteria based on this kind of analysis. When English teachers seek to assess their pupils' writing, they are very often looking for literary qualities, but they are also, inevitably, affected by the linguistic properties of the

the writing. We would argue, therefore, that it is important for teachers to make explicit for themselves the linguistic as well as the literary attributes of pupils' writing which constitute the real criteria in their assessments. However, most of these considerations affect assessment in the upper secondary rather than the middle school range.

Up to the age of 13 two considerations should be uppermost. One is the need for children to write because they want to. If there must be examinations, or tests, let them set tasks which children respond to. The other is the need for their writing to have a basic efficiency in handling sentence patterns and vocabulary for a variety of purposes. As we have emphasized elsewhere, this does not imply formal instruction in sentence-making, although children may sometimes need help in working out how to say what they want to say—but making sure they want to say it is much more important.

The marking of examinations should follow the principle outlined earlier in this chapter, that close marking is a waste of effort unless subsequent use is going to be made of it. It is now unusual for English specialists to try to allocate essay marks by elements which cannot really be separated, such as 'ideas' and 'originality'. They have found that it does not work, and very much the same applies to allocating marks for spelling, punctuation, and other elements of this kind. Such sub-divisions make marking-schemes too inflexible. It is fairer, and easier, to use a single impression mark, and to ask for a colleague to review the scripts if there is any doubt about the consistency of the marking. English is often the only subject in which pupils cannot obtain full marks, which seems to us very odd.

Chapter 8

Points of debate

In previous chapters we have touched on some controversial questions, or have implied our attitudes toward them, and will doubtless have led some readers to wonder what we would have to say about this, that, or the other 'key' question about English teaching. While it is not possible to predict all the issues on which we might be questioned, the obvious ones which arise in any discussion among, for example, junior school teachers, are easily predictable. In this chapter we want to confront these 'basic' issues as firmly as we can. In doing so, we are concerned only partly to justify our own positions, because there are some issues where we remain resolutely neutral. We are concerned also to help every English teacher by providing some of the defences for the general approach we have advocated. Most people think of the English teacher as the teacher who always says 'Don't . . .'. Most teachers think of English teachers as those who are called upon to ensure that children write neatly, spell correctly, read fluently, think logically, speak courteously, and, by speaking and writing correctly according to the current standards of correctness, eventually pass their English examinations. Laymen and parents generally bear on all teachers with this set of expectations, and many teachers in turn bear on their colleagues who teach English. The English teacher is therefore in an exposed position in staffrooms as well as classrooms. If he is in need of defences, we hope he may find parts of this chapter useful.

Literacy and illiteracy
The seemingly simple but quite devastating set of expectations of English teaching listed in the previous paragraph conceals two deep-seated fallacies. One we have already mentioned: the idea that English has a content which can be learned in a simple, linear fashion like, say, Euclidean geometry. The other is perhaps more serious. It is the feeling that deficiency in language skills is somehow a social or moral defect, as well as an educational or cognitive one. To put this another way, the common use of the term

'illiterate' as a damning social label suggests that this is an aspect of
schooling about which many people have very strong prejudices.

In one sense, of course, to be illiterate in an advanced industrial society
is a very serious deficiency indeed. The proportion of jobs requiring no degree
of literacy at all is declining very rapidly all the time, and there is nobody
who is entirely safe, physically, without being able to read a bare minimum
of warnings. Nobody needs to be told this, least of all the English teacher,
who knows better than most how intractable real illiteracy can be after
childhood. But life is made needlessly difficult for English teachers by the
free use of the term 'illiterate' as a label for almost anything in a piece of
writing that the reader happens to dislike strongly. There are many teachers
who have spent long hours teaching a wholly illiterate child to read and
write, and have had their efforts set at nought by a colleague who has
inspected the child's early, halting efforts at continuous writing and dis-
missed them, to his face, as 'illiterate'. Again, English teachers are used to
being approached by colleagues with some choice example of a child's
error and a trigger-happy firing of some broad rhetorical question—'Haven't
you taught 4B to write decent English yet?' English teachers sometimes
engage in the same shifting of responsibility when they blame primary
schools for allowing some, or even any, children to move up to the secondary
school without being able to read. But the matter of literacy is much more
complicated than this sort of labelling suggests. In lay usage, 'illiterate' can
mean anything from the total inability to decode written symbols to an
indisposition to insert commas, or apostrophes, or sentence boundaries, in
the places where a particular reader has been brought up to put them himself. So we must begin by making some necessary, basic distinctions between
these terms, as they are technically used.

Literate: able to achieve a reading age of 9·0 on tests devised for the purpose
of measuring the reading age of children.

Semi-literate: able to score a reading age between 7·0 and 9·0.

Illiterate: unable to achieve a reading age score of 7·0 years.

The tests of reading age, and the scales on which their results are expressed
regard literacy as the condition of the normal child of 9·0 years. However,
most of these tests are now some decades old, and are out of date in two ways.
The actual attainment of the total population of this country's children has
moved upwards, so that the real average reading age for children of 9 is several
months higher than 9·0. Secondly, the words chosen for these tests include a
number which have gone wholly out of use ('mannequin' is a well-known
example), and we strongly suspect that there is enough of this obsolescence
in the tests to have made most reading age scores quite invalid. It was a report

based on such tests which led to the Inquiry into the Teaching of Reading and the Use of English, the report of which was written at the same time as this book. (See K.B. Start and R.B. Wells, *The Trend of Reading Standards*, National Foundation for Educational Research, 1971.) In our view some (but not all) of the anxiety behind the setting up of the Bullock Inquiry, as it has become known, was quite groundless.

There is a further sense in which reading age scores are not very helpful to English teachers. Like other statistical phenomena, they are distributed over a wide range. In a normal population of children aged 11, the reading age scores will range all the way from less than 7·0 to over 15; and the proportion of 11 year olds with reading ages below 9·0 must, by definition, be well over 10%. It is therefore quite unrealistic to expect the primary school system not only to improve on this figure (as it seems to have done over much of the country) but also to go on improving average performance indefinitely. In any case, the focus of concern about reading standards, on the best recent evidence, lies not in primary but in secondary schools. Finally, a major factor in reading performance is the motivation of the pupil, but his attitudes may also affect his performance in tests.

Reading age scores, too, are based on tests which rely on responses to individual words. From a linguistic viewpoint this is naive: language is much more than words taken individually. A reading age score tells us nothing about the ability to interpret continuous text, or about the ability to write– and laymen are much more ready to judge the literacy of children on their writing than on their reading. Nor can a reading age score tell us anything about the aspect of language which in the long run is decisive, the mastery of spoken language. Teachers of infants are generally well aware that a child who *does not* say very much at the age of 5 may have a very adequate mastery of the spoken language, either as a listener or, when he wishes, as a speaker; but the child of 5 who *cannot* express himself orally when he wants to is likely to need special educational help very soon. (See B. Cane and J. Smithers, *The Roots of Reading*, National Foundation for Educational Research, 1971). Even so, infant teachers know that children learn different things very differently: in infant, junior, and secondary stages mastery of reading and mastery of writing may be gained at different times, at different speeds, and through different kinds of learning activities.[1] Areas of learning which may seem related to the adult may be quite out of phase with each other for children. Just as there is a wide contrast, in most children, between the vocabulary they normally use and that which they can respond to, so there is a wide range of contrast between different levels of reading skill. We need to go far beyond the notion of literacy, and to think in terms of

the next stage. This we shall call reading competence, and in turn distinguish
it from writing competence.

Reading competence

The section on language development at the end of Chapter 2 summarizes
many of the things which a child has to learn in the course of moving from
being literate (in the technical sense) to being a competent reader. Here we
want to suggest three approaches which may help children in this process.
They need to be brought to realize, as soon as is reasonably possible, that reading can be *fun*. The only way to do this is to provide them with free access to
books which they can read and which they will also very much enjoy—and
we mean enjoy with glee, relish, zest, or quiet conviction. Many children
who have had a struggle with learning to read in the first place have met a
landmark in their lives when they came across Spike Milligan's *Silly Verse
for Kids* (Puffin) or Michael Bond's Paddington books (Armada). Books like
the B.B.C.'s Jackanory series, too, can follow up the great enjoyment many
deprived children obtain from their television viewing. The story book
which absorbs a child's complete attention is an essential element in
his imaginative growth, but it is far more than that: it is a vitally necessary
exposure to sustained, continuous written language. In reading such stories
as Ted Hughes' *The Iron Man* (Faber), E.B. White's *Charlotte's Web* (Puffin),
or Clive King's *Stig of the Dump* (Puffin), a child of 9 or 10 is not only
enjoying himself: he is also acquiring a developed reading competence. The
teacher needs to know about the books, and ideally to have read some of
them; to see that they are available; and to stir interest by reading occasional
chapters. He should not be surprised, however, if some of his chosen books
do not go down well.

A second approach in helping children to move beyond literacy to
competence as readers involves an effort to narrow the gap between the
written language of the books and the spoken language of the pupils. This
is very obvious in teaching foreign languages (witness the remark of an 11
year old on a bus in Exeter: 'Us be learning French us be.'). But if the contrast
between written and spoken language is too great, the reader of a story will
never achieve a satisfactory 'interior performance' of it. The need to bridge
this gap calls for some sustained reading aloud, especially by the teacher
from texts which include conversation, and for other approaches outlined
in Chapter 4. Teachers who do not read aloud well in the classroom can use
a tape-recorder at leisure, or can draw on regular broadcasts. Some teachers'
centres have developed banks of cassetted story-readings, and these can and
should include some very short and simple stories for children whose previous

exposure to spoken language has been impoverished. Some such children will listen to these repeatedly with a visible hunger for the pleasure and learning they have thus far gone without.

Thirdly, one of the reasons why children do not move easily from the security of reading simple sentences aloud word by word to the less familiar territory of extension readers or complete novels is sheer inattention. Many children are superficial readers, and can become more so if they are encouraged to 'get through' a book rather than read it. An approach which forestalls this is the use of very simple work-cards designed to make the pupil read some or even most of the text again. To take two simple examples of this kind of task:

Make a list of the main characters in the first three chapters of *Charlotte's Web*, and write three or four sentences describing each of them.

Imagine that Stig (in *Stig of the Dump*) and the boy who found him had both been girls. Write your version of their first meeting.

Writing competence

Most teachers take it for granted that children will read rather better than they write. But they are apt to think of 'writing' as a single skill. In fact it is a very complex set of quite distinct skills, some motor, some cognitive, and some perceptual. 'Writing' requires a recognition knowledge of letter shapes, the ability to manipulate the writing instrument, the spatial perception of relationships between script and paper, the ability to form the letter shapes, and form them into meaningful sequences ... and so the list could go on. And individual children will need to learn different skills at different stages. The teacher of children under 13 may always need to start by establishing his pupils' level of attainment in these multiple skills, in order to plan out a realistic programme of work. As so often, this means being clear about the objectives involved.

Any sample of the writing of children aged between 9 and 13 will provide a body of material which can be assessed in two ways. A search for qualities of honesty, candour, sincerity, and care for the written product is something made—this literary evaluation is one kind, and it is entirely legitimate. A search for evidence of what learning tasks face the children who have produced the writing is less literary in spirit, but it is just as important, although rather more difficult because most teachers are not trained to do it. The kind of 'error-analysis' which lies behind the 'grammar and usage'

elements of course books is of two kinds: the writers have collected sets of
items which children often leave out of written text, and have set up exercises designed to teach them what to insert and where; or they have looked
at the simple syntax of children's writing and tried to set up exercises
showing them how to use a more complex set of structures. The majority
of 'missing item' exercises concern punctuation, which we shall discuss in
a moment. Exercises in syntax rest on the assumption that children are
using very simple structures because they do not have any others, but the
relationship between meaning and syntax is more complicated than this
allows for. Fundamentally children will select syntactic forms to match
what they want to say, as all of us do, from the range of forms with which
they are familiar. The key to the problem, therefore, lies in the range of
forms with which they are familiar, and this brings us back once more to
the scale and depth of their extensive reading. One might almost go so far
as to say that in the 9 to 13 age range much English teaching has the
balance between reading and writing the wrong way round: in this period
it is the reading which should have priority, because it is from the reading
that children will become familiar with the syntactic resources of the
written language.

A policy for spelling

Language is learned by using it. This 'doing' is a two-way process of trans-
posing written symbols into messages and vice-versa. The complexity of
the writing system of English is so great that there have been many attempts
to provide simplified versions, from Bell's Visible Speech to the Initial
Teaching Alphabet. These Special Writing Systems, as they are known, do
not and cannot solve the basic educational problem, because almost everything in writing which a child's education is fitting him to deal with is in
the traditional orthography, or TO.

From a linguistic point of view, however, the TO is very much less of a
mess than Shaw and his many followers have believed. We have to distinguish
between symbols, the labels given to them, and the sounds to which the
symbols correspond. On this basis, the twenty-six letters of the conventional
alphabet are *labels*, and they label only a part of the set of symbols available
in English. Other symbols in our writing system, which are not equipped with
alphabetical labels in this way, include *th*, *ch*, *sh*, and all the complex symbols which combine more than one vowel symbol, such as *ei*, *eau*, or *au*. But
there is a further complication: not only do we have many more symbols
than the letters of the alphabet; but the language uses more than one symbol
to correspond to one sound (compare *I* with *eye*, for instance) and can also

use different symbols to correspond to one sound (compare *duty* with *beauty*, or the first and last consonants in *judge*). These complications may seem to be quite without rhyme or reason, but close analysis has shown that the writing system is in general regular. (See K.A. Albrow, *The English Writing System: notes toward a description*, Longman, Papers in Linguistics and English Teaching Series II.) The regularities may be very complicated, like the system of cases in Russian or Finnish, but they are there. They arise from several sources. One is the nature of syllable structure in English. Another is the visual differentiation of words which sound alike. We rarely, if ever, have any doubt in speech whether someone is saying *sight* or *site*, but in a written text we need the help of the spelling to be certain. Another important aspect of English spelling is that it has to cater for an astonishing range of variations in accent, and for the great number of derived forms in the language. (For example, the final symbol in *roar* seems superfluous, until we hear a Scotsman or need to use the derived form *roaring*.) The truth of the matter is that English spelling is not the confusion it is widely thought to be. It has no need whatever for the false etymologists who attributed (for example) the *b* in *debt* to the Latin *debeo*. The study of etymology, whether true or false, has been part of the lore and language of schoolmasters for generations, but is of no help whatever to the average pupil's spelling.

All this means that the English system of spelling is complicated because it has a complicated job to do—servicing, so to speak, an immense variety of regional and dialectal forms of speech. The complications are so great, however, that the sum total of simple 'spelling rules' which can be learned in school do not add up to any really significant proportion of the regular patterns actually in use. The great majority of our spelling system has to be learned in some other way. Now, infants learn spoken language by assimilation from their speech environment. Older children can be expected, with help, to assimilate written language from their written language environment. This points directly to the programme of a language-enriched classroom—extensive reading, word-gaming, and 'hooking up' written language to speech—that we have already outlined. Thus, children will not learn that *height* and *weight* correspond to different vowel sounds unless, as well as knowing the words in the spoken language, they *also* meet them in written words. The number of these correspondences between sound and symbol in English is so great, and the rules which they follow are so abstract, that a policy of saturating children in written-text-brought-to-sound and spoken-language-brought-to-page will be far more productive than reliance on rules or rote-learning of spellings. The limited research in this field firmly supports

this view. (See M. Peters, *Spelling—Caught or Taught?*, Routledge, and
C. Chomsky, 'Reading, Writing, and Phonology', in Frank Smith,
Psycholinguistics and Reading, Holt, Rinehart, and Winston.)

This does not mean that there is no place for rote-learning at all. Its
place is in dealing with children's mistakes—but even here one needs to be
selective. Spelling mistakes are of three distinct kinds: new words not yet
mastered, habitual errors, and carelessness or haste. New words not yet
mastered reflect the language learning of the class in a revealing way, and
work on their spelling needs caution if the learning is not to be discour-
aged. But the habitual error, especially of the sort which goes back to
look-and-say methods of teaching reading, with all the inattention to
individual letters that they involve, has to be put right by the corrective
therapy of spelling tests and rote-learning. The old-fashioned spelling test
can be handled inventively, just like any other traditional procedure. For
example, one can collect up a score of spelling errors from a set of compositions and write the correct words on the board (since it should not be
taken for granted that children of 11 can use dictionaries easily). The class
has its test next day, and is then asked to use all twenty words in a story
in any order they like—and many a class will turn this into a competition
to see who can do it most economically. A natural extension is into derived
forms—the adjective, adverb, and verb derived from the root noun, for
example—in which English is very rich. The affixation-game, of attaching
as many prefixes and suffixes as a stem will bear, is another version which
attracts many children and gives them much unconscious repetition of
easily mis-spelled words, as well as insight into the mechanics of derivation.
In the long run, however, children will spell if their teachers make clear
that good spelling is one of the things they expect. To expect anything
less, in a society which attaches weight to spelling, is to deceive them about
the real world.

Punctuation

The rules about spelling, however complicated, are definite, even though
they change over time. But with punctuation one mans habit is another
mans anathema, and it is very easy not to notice variations. (For example,
many readers will have missed the two omitted apostrophes in the previous
sentence.) On the whole, this book has been written with a fairly 'heavy'
punctuation: we have used commas and colons and semi-colons to try to
make our meaning clearer. There are many writers of very reputable English
who use much less punctuation and easily accustom their readers to very
long sentences which have virtually no punctuation of any significance

between the full-stops marking the boundaries between sentences (like this one). Similarly, there are readers who go through any lightly punctuated text mentally putting in the commas. For literate adults, then, punctuation is something which writer and reader come to terms about. For children, the same basic argument applies as we have used about written text in general: children cannot learn punctuation out of thin air. They need sustained and intensive exposure to punctuated written text. In a word, they need to read. But there is a little more to it than this, because punctuation has a dual function. It marks off the main syntactic segments of a sentence, and marks off one sentence from another; but it also acts as a set of cues for the 'interior performance' of a text that we mentioned earlier. Any good reader, reading aloud well, knows that a colon calls for a particular pattern in his use of pitch, and the same applies to semi-colons, paired or parenthetic commas, and many other uses of punctuation. This once more points to a powerful role for reading aloud in the English class, and especially, of course, for reading aloud which has been prepared or rehearsed.

The writing of the vast majority of children between 9 and 13, however, will be satisfactorily punctuated if they can master a central feature of written English. This is the sentence boundary. The segments of spoken discourse in English are in reality not at all the same as the sentences of written English, and it is probably unfruitful to treat them as if they were. Many young children narrate orally with strings of clauses breathlessly strung together with *and* or *then*. Much of their early writing will reflect this. Most children, however, will learn alternative ways of structuring their spoken discourse only very slowly. Learning to segment their written discourse into sentences will depend largely on their exposure to written language, but, as we have suggested in several places, the two areas of learning can influence one another and cross-fertilization should be encouraged. The teacher who reads aloud well to his class is teaching, among other things, how to handle the patterns by which written English segments its discourse. Statements are usually marked by a falling pitch at the end, and questions by a rising pitch, and so on. Very little is known about this aspect of language learning, but our understanding of language suggests very strongly that having good models is much more instructive than any number of exercises. Trying to teach the 'right' places for full-stops by asking children to slot them into a written text does nothing to tell them what makes the places 'right'. Reading the passage aloud will always help. The same will often apply to children's own writing, especially if they have been allowed to slip into the bad habit of writing first and punctuating a whole passage afterwards.

Punctuation is an integral part of meaning, and as is clear from an inspection of the diverse habits of great writers it is very variable. (See P.S.Doughty *et al*, *Exploring Language*, Edward Arnold, Chapter 9.) It is far too important to be made the victim of pointless over-teaching or over-anxious pedantry. Perhaps the most glaring instance of over-teaching is the punctuation of direct speech: a set of increasingly empty conventions which is apt to be taught in every school year from the age of 7 to the age of 16, with what must, on that evidence, be very poor success. There is no need to teach children to *write* fully punctuated direct speech in the junior school at all, but the pressure of convention and anxiety will doubtless keep it going. The *paragraphing* of direct speech is of course quite another matter. However, to teach children to write it before they have had long exposure to reading it is bound to be confusing. If it has to be taught in a formal way, the 'balloons' of speech in comic strips can be very useful raw material for pupils to work on. One classic case of pedantry in this field is the apostrophe, which written English can happily do without. The paired commas which denote a parenthesis, on the other hand, are much more often necessary for the sense of a passage, and, if taught against a background of how the sound gives the clue to the punctuation, relatively easy to teach. Even more arbitrary than the rules about the apostrophe is the insistence on 'full' form for the punctuating of letters and addresses—when the Department of Education and Science itself has adopted the 'clean' form without commas and full stops.

Dyslexia

The complexity of language means that a particular breakdown in learning it may arise from a very wide variety of causes. This in turn means that serious breakdown may be very difficult to diagnose properly and seemingly impossible to treat. In the case of reading, serious learning difficulties of distinct kinds very easily become confused, and in recent years it has become fashionable to label this pattern of multiple difficulty with the term 'dyslexia'. Strictly speaking this is a diagnosis of an inability of the nervous system to process the recognition of letter shapes, and the older term 'word blindness' probably gives a more accurate picture of the problem. Accordingly, 'dyslectic' is a term which should be used only by a trained diagnostician or educational psychologist. In any other usage it is almost certainly inaccurate and may be misleading: the genuine dyslectic is quite rare, and to use this label for other, more soluble problems may hinder their solution. The widespread parental concern about dyslexia reflects a concern about all the reading difficulties which tend to come under the same label, and this interest is of immense value to teachers—provided it serves to focus attention on children who need help (whether dyslectics or not), and provided it does not lead to amateur attempts to solve highly technical problems. Another aspect of this concern affects all parental pressure groups: individual parents need to exercise great care to ensure that the anxieties of their own children are not increased by parental activity.[2]

Handwriting

Most infant and junior schools tackle the initial years of reading and writing with a combination of printed books and a clear, round script for classroom labels and work-books which is also echoed in many printed materials. The children naturally adopt this script themselves, and up to the point where they have learned to link letters together they are encouraged in it. At that stage an extraordinary number of schools feel obliged to undo all this good work by giving lessons in handwriting which set out to impose a formalized script. In some cases this is a form of italic, which requires special pens, devoted teaching, uniformity among a staff, and a thorough, trained understanding of the technique. In other cases, which we have found rather more numerous, the script chosen is what is loosely called 'looped'—a simplified, upright version of what used to be known as copperplate. The systematic imposition of italic script can be made to work, at a price. The attempt to convert every child to 'looped' script almost invariably fails, chiefly because as a style it has neither theoretical justification nor aesthetic appeal. Either policy is fundamentally aiming at getting children to behave, in respect of handwriting, like much older people. The cost in confusion to many children is high, and the necessary corporate pressure of a whole staff over several years is in practice very difficult to achieve.

Handwriting is a motor skill rather than a linguistic one. Like all other motor skills in childhood it develops through constant use over a long period. It develops best if it is subject, throughout that period and from all sources, to a steady pressure for better performance, which does not cause anxiety. A complex motor skill does not become habitual until the neural and motor system of the individual is mature—i.e., in most people, after puberty or later. The idea that this process can be short-circuited by instruction in the junior school is pure fantasy. The time spent on it would be much more usefully devoted to the creative art and craft work which calls for the children's utmost control of hands and fingers without making them tense with worry. The severely untidy writer is almost always a child with other difficulties, emotional or cognitive, anyway. The majority of children, allowed to follow their own bent within a general requirement for clarity and economy, will develop a matured script between the ages of 12 and 15.

One aspect of this maturity is that the script reflects the writer's individuality, and in one sense its development is an integral part of the adolescent's establishment of his own identity. During this phase some children will naturally experiment—with coloured ink in exercise books, or with adventurous posters and display work, for example. Such experiments are not merely trying out the limits of what is allowed: like a serious attempt to adopt, say, italic by an otherwise co-operative pupil, they should be encouraged.

There usually comes a point in children's school careers, most commonly in the second or third year of secondary school, when the pressures of time and work impose severe strain on a child's ability to write with sufficient speed. A quite normal response to this situation is the development of two distinct scripts—a private, 'fast' one for notes and rough drafts, and a more public or formal one for fair copies.The problem is obvious: does the fast script become tidy enough for public use, or can it influence the formal script so as to make it fast enough for general use? In practice the former happens in the vast majority of cases, and schools which treat this rapid script, and the temporary untidiness which its use involves, with strong disapproval may be hindering rather than helping. But they will not be hindering their pupils anything like so severely as the school which deprives them of ruled pages in their exercise books. Surprisingly, there are still schools which retain this quaint relic of the past; they imagine that the awkward problems which children have with handwriting are actually helped by the compulsory use of unlined exercise-books with a line-guide behind the page. It is a most effective and foolish sabotage of English teaching, since it removes all freedom to select the medium according to the needs of the task. Files for unlined or lined paper, provided as the task requires, serve the need well and respect the teacher's professional freedom.

'Correct English'

Some readers may still wonder, after what we have said about the diversity of English, and about the differences between spoken and written English, whether we are not selling the pass about standards altogether. In fact, of course, there is no single, standard 'correct' English: the imperative verb addressed to the reader is incorrect in academic prose, while any other might be incorrect in advertising copy. This is why there has been so strong a move away from simplistic ideas of correctness to the much more flexible idea of appropriateness. But the use of appropriateness as a criterion for judging a pupil's writing is not, in itself, a flabby weakness: an informal letter has to be just as good in its spelling as a formal essay, and its punctuation may even have to be better. It really does matter that teachers should develop a more sophisticated awareness of language than the pedantry which, for example, bans all use of the first person pronoun, or wastes time insisting, Canute-like, that contemporary English has not accepted *onto* as a single word. Language is a social phenomenon, and we live in a society where pedants-in-office still abound, so it is no service to children to let them think that mechanical accuracy in their writing does not matter. But every English teacher needs to mediate between the vast weight of this social pressure and the learning which his pupils are capable of at the precise time he has to teach them.

Relations with colleagues
Schools in England mark the boundary between classrooms, as a rule, very firmly. The boundary is usually both the physical one of walls and doors, and an acoustic one, in the form of an assumption that one teacher's activity does not make such noise as will obtrude on another class. There is also an important but invisible boundary between subjects in the curriculum. The English teacher will usually make every possible accommodation to colleagues in the matter of noise—drama work and discussion in groups do not have to annoy neighbouring teachers. The English teacher also has little occasion to cross the subject boundaries and suggest what should or should not be done in mathematics or history lessons. Unfortunately the reverse is not so true: because teachers of other subjects are also native speakers of English, they are apt to think they know the English teacher's job better than he does. The proper professional response to this situation is a quality of cohesion within an English department, or between the teacher best qualified in the work and the colleagues who look to him for guidance. Thus, the secondary school head of department who allows much of his own subject to be taught by non-specialists, and does not also secure regular departmental discussion of their work and problems, is putting them in an unfair position.

Beyond this, however, language learning is taking place in every subject, and the school is thus a language environment in which all teachers play some part, whether they recognize this or not.

Immigrant pupils
The very existence of this book implies that we believe non-specialists can teach English quite competently. Indeed, many already do so with distinction: they think out what they are doing, draw on expert practice, and

contribute one of the many kinds of English teaching for which the profession has room. But such teaching is concerned with children whose native language is British English. The teaching of a foreign language is quite another matter, and it is too easily forgotten that for many immigrant children English is just that. Moreover, having a formal qualification in English in a native speaker context no more equips the English specialist to teach it as a foreign language than it does the art or mathematics specialist. English with immigrants, that is to say, is a specialism within a specialism.

There has been much discussion about the official definition of 'immigrant' pupils as those whose families have lived in Britain for less than ten years. It is a legitimate rule of thumb, but oversimplifies a complicated picture. For example, many Uganda Asians speak (either bilingually or as a native language) an English which is relatively close to British English. West Indians, on the other hand, speak West Indian English, which in its spoken form has marked differences from British speech. In both cases the language of the home may well be supportive of an education conducted in British English. Many Indian and Pakistani families, however, continue to use their native languages (which are many and widely varied) at home, and the educational problem for their children is of a quite different order.

One of the greatest sources of difficulty for both teachers and learners in this context lies in the nature of speech sounds. The range of sounds employed in human language is well over a hundred, but any one language will not normally use more than forty or fifty of them, and any two languages may have very few sounds indeed in common. Furthermore the human ear trains itself to hear those sounds which it is used to much more acutely than unfamiliar ones. A group of sixth-formers taught by one of the authors, for example, set out to identify the speech sounds of Gujerati, and discovered very few that they recognized. In order to identify and describe others it was necessary to learn some phonetics. In order to identify all the sounds of a language accurately requires intensive and highly skilled training, as does also the process of learning to speak them accurately. This is why numerous European immigrants to Britain who came in the 1930s still speak English, nearly forty years later, with audibly foreign accents. In reality the foreign learner who acquires a phonetically perfect command of a language is very rare indeed, and the foreigner who can acquire even a working knowledge of it unaided is also rare. The immigrant child whose family continue to speak their native language at home cannot hope to master the medium of his whole education without sustained, skilled, intensive instruction.

The importance of this will be obvious to every teacher. The child's ability to interact in the classroom is governed by his powers of language, and lack of such ability will sooner or later alienate him from school altogether. Linguistic deficiencies which are less obviously noticeable in the classroom may play a very significant role in a pupil's success or failure without any of those involved being aware of them. This is why the discovery that West Indian children occupy a very disproportionate share of places in remedial classes and E.S.N. schools in some areas is so disturbing: educational failure which in reality arises from linguistic weakness is only too easily attributed to lack of ability or emotional disturbance. The tendency of some schools to lump linguistic deficiencies together with all other kinds of retardation or subnormality and consign the whole set of problems to the remedial department only compounds the problem.

It is also urgently necessary that teachers and heads dealing with immigrant pupils recognize that there are two major levels to the language problem. One is the elementary level of the business of getting along in the primary school's daily routine. The other is the (linguistically) quite different level of the requirements of the secondary school curriculum. Consider for example the simple point that in geometry one does not *draw* anything: one has to *construct* a circle, *describe* an arc, *erect* a perpendicular, *bisect* an angle, and so forth. These terms are so much a part of the thinking and the way of speaking of the mathematics teacher that he does not always pause to realize that every one of them may be unfamiliar to 11 year olds coming into secondary school and may need to be taught not once but several times. The immigrant pupil lacks the wider knowledge of the language and the cultural context which native children can draw on for help with such terms. And as we have stressed in Chapter 2, the total linguistic burden of the secondary curriculum can be enormous. It is small wonder that for many immigrant pupils the shock effect of transfer to secondary school is serious. Paradoxically, it seems that this effect is more marked in pupils who have undergone intensive language instruction on entry to primary school than in those who have not. The linguistic shock effect of going to secondary school has never been adequately investigated, although there are indications of its possible effects to be found in much of the literature about streaming and on the sociology of the secondary school. (For example, R. Lacey, *Hightown Grammar*, Manchester University Press, or D.H. Hargreaves, *Social Relations in a Secondary School*, Routledge.)

There is of course a wider issue of policy for Local Education Authorities. Relatively few L.E.A.s have grasped the magnitude of the language-learning problem in immigrant communities, and some of those have been frustrated by the natural desire of such groups to maintain their identity and resist assimilation. But when the scale of the need is recognized, its logic leads Authorities quite ineluctibly to special centres for intensive instruction. This is because there are simply not enough competent teachers of English as a foreign language to go round. Even if there were, to equip each and every school with the necessary facilities would be quite uneconomic and could prove short-sighted. There is considerable evidence that the need for special centres of language instruction has declined as the rate of immigration itself declined. This does not mean that immigrant pupils no longer present problems—and those problems may well be just as intractable as the initial language instruction one was. However, these are educational questions, and should be kept quite distinct from the issue of dispersal or 'bussing'.

The untrained non-specialist facing a class where numerous immigrants speak, understand, and read English badly has an insoluble problem. Approaching it with naive notions will only make it worse. For instance, many English people still suppose that a foreigner's competence at anything, and with language in particular, is best measured by his grasp not of his own language but of English. The notion that people are dim because they don't speak English well is still quite common but rarely admitted—perhaps because to admit it is to reveal its stupidity. Again, laymen measure someone's grasp of a language by how well he speaks it, as though hearing it and understanding it did not have to come first. Another set of naive notions concerns learning the sounds of English: children are often asked to pronounce sounds which they have not yet learned to hear accurately (such as the difference between -*dge* and -*tch*); they are asked to pronounce sounds on the basis of written sym bols rather than sounds in the ear; the sounds of English are taught to many immigrant children solely in their emphatic form, as though the native English always pronounce a hard *g* at the end of every word ending with -*ing* and always pronounce the vowel in *the*. These brief indications of just how easy it is to mislead pupils about the nature of our speech may perhaps suffice to show that this work does require some specialist knowledge. Fortunately it has been brought together, with valuable guidance to teachers, by a Schools Council project led by June Derrick, under the title *Scope*: the output of this project is substantial, including many teaching materials, and some particularly helpful background in *Scope Handbook 1* and *Scope Handbook 2* (Longman for Books for Schools Ltd).

Chapter 9

Theories and attitudes

Background

In previous chapters we have referred to the inquiry into English teaching under the chairmanship of Sir Alan Bullock which at the time of writing is nearing the completion of its work. The disquiet about reading standards which lay behind the appointment of this Committee is to some extent an inevitable consequence of a period of rapid expansion in the educational system. Employers of graduates are drawing on some 20% of the population going through the system, whereas twenty-five years ago the figure was about 5%. The proportion of school leavers expected by society to have a high degree of literacy is in reality immeasurably greater than at any previous time in our history. It is against this background of steady and, in recent years, very rapid expansion that the history of English teaching, its attitudes and theoretical positions, should be understood. We do not propose to write such a history here, but the serious non-specialist is entitled to ask for basic guidance about the principal landmarks of the past few decades. Our purpose in this chapter is to sketch in this kind of orientation, indicating the more significant movements and suggesting where some of the more useful additional guidance may be found.

The report of the Bullock Committee will be the first document of its kind for half a century. The only other full-scale official inquiry into the teaching of English in this country was set up in 1919 under the chairmanship of Sir Henry Newbolt, and its Report makes a convenient starting point for this brief survey. We should remember that at that date relatively few children in secondary schools were of less than considerable ability, and that the grammar schools of the time were still deeply affected by the traditional priority of classical studies, which had received strong support from Sir Robert Morant and other senior officers of the Board of Education. The Newbolt Report (H.M.S.O.), however, was quite unequivocal:

> For English children no form of knowledge can take precedence of a
> knowledge of English, no form of literature can take precedence of
> English literature: and . . . the two are so inextricably connected as to
> form the only basis possible for a national education. (Para.9.)

The Report is equally plain about what this means:

> English, we are convinced, must form the essential basis of a liberal
> education for all English people, and in the earlier stages of education
> it should be the principal function of all schools of whatever type to
> provide this basis.
> Of this provision the component parts will be, first, systematic
> training in the sounded speech of standard English, to secure correct
> pronunciation and clear articulation; second, systematic training in the
> use of standard English, to secure clearness and correctness both in oral
> expression and in writing: third, training in reading. Under this last
> head will be included reading aloud with feeling and expression, the use
> of books as sources of information and study, and finally, the use of
> literature as we have already described it, that is, as a possession and a
> source of delight, a personal intimacy and the gaining of a personal
> experience, an end in itself and, at the same time, an equipment for the
> understanding of life. (Para.13.)

One does not expect official reports to emerge with radical conclusions,
but the implicit rejection of classical studies is decisive. The results,
unhappily, were less sound than the intentions. We may see readily how,
in the passage just quoted, the notions of a 'standard English' and of
'correctness' are firmly entrenched, as if English were a language which
could be studied in some ideal form. The idea of continuing change and
growth in a living language, the conception of varieties within the language,
and the contrasts between spoken language and written language—these
wholly escape the Committee. One consequence was a marked increase in
the teaching of prescriptive English grammar and style, from which we are
only now beginning to escape. Moreover, as the phrase about 'component
parts' suggests, the Report reinforced the fragmented English curriculum
described in our opening chapter. The dependence of the schools on the
system of public examinations gave particular weight to the Examination
Boards' readiness to follow the more prescriptive recommendations and
ignore others. Thus, 'English should be compulsory to the extent of
including, either in the form of précis or otherwise, a test of the power to
grasp the meaning of a piece of English of appropriate difficulty.' In the
light of the standard reliance of the Boards on formal précis, the 'or
otherwise' remained a pious gesture. Other recommendations are still not
entirely implemented to this day:

93.   That an examination on set books should leave the teacher of
       literature as free as possible to draw up his own syllabus and to
       adopt his own methods.

95.   That oral examination should be resorted to more frequently.

While, therefore, the Newbolt Report did little to change the daily practice
of English teaching, especially in grammar schools, it did bring about a
vitally important change in the status of the subject. This created a career
structure for the English graduates of the new civic universities, and brought
into being a body of specialist teachers. This in turn had a significant effect
on educational opportunities for girls, since English studies attracted them
in increasing numbers. The private sector largely ignored these changes,
however, and it was not until after 1960 that some of the most eminent
public schools appointed their first specialist English teachers.

Among the witnesses who gave evidence to the Newbolt Committee was
Caldwell Cook, who represented a conception of English teaching which
went far beyond what the Committee was prepared to endorse. Cook
taught English at the Perse School in Cambridge, and had published *The
Play Way* (Heinemann) as early as 1917. This book, whose title has been
much misrepresented since, makes an astonishing case for grounding the
curriculum in the needs and interests of children rather than in pre-conceived
notions of 'the subject'. Cook laid enormous emphasis on the importance of
motivation. The kind of absorbed, committed engagement in a rigorous and
intellectually demanding activity which Cook sought to generate in his
pupils (and which by all accounts he succeeded in creating) was so novel a
departure that it had no adequate label. For it, Cook chose the term 'play',
drawing both on the analogy of young children totally absorbed in constructive activity and on the dramatic impact of theatrical experience, on
either side of the curtain. It was to become an unfortunate label in later
years, but Cook's experiments in the teaching of Shakespeare underlie
most subsequent developments in educational drama, and his writing shows
a grasp of the psychology of intuitive learning which is far from out-dated.
Cook was one of the earliest educators to see the value of children's own
creative work, and the fact that his teaching was with intelligent and well-
motivated pupils makes only a minor difference to its importance.

George Sampson, a member of the Newbolt Committee, produced in
his now famous book *English for the English* (C.U.P., 1921) a re-statement of
views which find expression in a much watered-down form in the Report
itself. His social assumptions as an educator are decades ahead of his time,
but he clearly understood the fact:

We must abandon our system of class education and find some form of education common to the schools of all classes. A common school is, at present, impracticable. We are not nearly ready yet to assimilate such a revolutionary change. But though a common school is impracticable, a common basis of education is not. The one common basis of a common culture is the common tongue. (p.39.)

Sampson puts forward a programme for a unified English teaching in which grammar is at a minimum and literature is at the centre. Above all, like Cook, he wanted teaching which related to the needs and interests of the pupils. It is a humane and heart-felt book, and a fortunate recent reprint (C.U.P., 1970) makes it accessible to every student.

While the Newbolt Committee was clearly influenced by views such as those of Cook and Sampson, and its Report had many virtues, it fell far short of the insights these two people brought to its work. This fact is even more evident in the subsequent course of events than in the pages of the Report. For in spite of the pleas for the unification of language and literature, English teaching in the ensuing two decades exhibited precisely this separation. Moreover, the contrast between the grammar schools, which taught the able and the children of ambitious parents, and the rest of the secondary system was one which teachers of the present generation would find unbelievable. The generous resources made available to the former meant that literature was accessible in them, while the mass of secondary pupils were confined to a nuts-and-bolts kind of English which cost much less and made it much easier to keep order. The almost unconscious assumption that this distinction was part of the order of nature finds echoes in the main educational documents of the whole period, whether the Hadow Report of 1926, the Spens Report of 1939, or, most tellingly of all, the Norwood Report of 1943 on which the structure of 11+ selection was to be erected after the war. It is no wonder that English teachers have tended to see their central professional debate as one between the advocates of literature and the supporters of grammar and correctness. But the two parties to the debate were on most occasions talking about different kinds of pupil in different kinds of school. The almost total absence of any serious university study of English as a language in this period contributed to the low status of language teaching.

The thirties and after
There emerged at the end of the 1930s, however, a clear sign of dissent. The achievement and influence of F.R. Leavis and his fellow contributors to *Scrutiny* during that decade are outside our present scope. Naturally

this influence embraced some teachers in schools, particularly in grammar and public schools. But to give this influence coherence, and to preserve among isolated teachers some sense of belonging to a significant professional group, was the task and the achievement of Denys Thompson. Beginning in 1939, and drawing strength and support from Boris Ford and other former students of F.R. Leavis, Thompson's journal *The Use of English* (originally *English in Schools*) was to provide, as it still does, the kind of exchange of critical commentary and classroom experience that no other non-scientific subject in the curriculum has had. Its influence was naturally greatest among grammar school teachers, many of whom formed themselves into local Use of English Groups. Denys Thompson conducted *The Use of English* with studied moderation: it resisted the temptation to become a conventional learned journal, and its cumulative effect was to render for English and its teachers the service which the Newbolt Report could not in its time contrive: it gave them a sense of profession. By comparison, most other subject-groups of teachers at the time and their journals were moribund.

In his own writings for sixth-forms and English teachers, Thompson consistently reflected the stance taken in F.R. Leavis' essay of 1930, *Mass Civilization and Minority Culture* (Gordon Fraser Minority Pamphlets):

> In any period it is upon a very small minority that the discerning appreciation of art and literature depends . . . Upon this minority depends our power of profiting by the finest human experience of the past; they keep alive the subtlest and most perishable parts of tradition. Upon them depend the implicit standards that order the finer living of the age.

Leavis and Thompson collaborated on a textbook, *Culture and Environment* (Chatto and Windus), published in 1933, which amongst other things set out to alert sixth-formers to the dangers of advertising but relied largely on advertisements invented for the purpose. A far better book, by Thompson alone, *Reading and Discrimination* (Chatto and Windus, 1934), set a style for literary studies by juxtaposing pairs of verse or prose passages and asking, quite simply, which was the better of the two. Both these books and the long editorship of *The Use of English*, all three of which were undeniably influential, were inspired by a concern for the quality of life. 'The quality of a man's life nowadays', he wrote in 1934, echoing Arnold, 'depends largely on the quality of what he reads.' The English teacher's task is to seek out and reinforce the cultural standards of the minority. This outlook was to prove enduring, and emerges in much more recent books. (For example, Denys Thompson (ed.), *Directions in the Teaching of English*, Chatto and Windus, 1969.) However seemingly noble the ideal of a minority which preserves culture from contamination by the popular and contemporary culture, its practical effect was to perpetuate a paternalistic and elitist position, and to drive in more firmly than ever the wedge between literature for the able and language for the rest.

By the 1960s, however, the demands of the secondary modern and the comprehensive school (almost George Sampson's common school) enforced an attention to equality as well as to quality. There was developing among many English teachers an urgent concern to extend to a much wider range of pupils the benefits of a literary education, coupled with a recognition that the pupils who could respond to serious literature were much more numerous than many teachers in selective schools had supposed. In 1964 the network of *Use of English* groups developed into the National Association for the Teaching of English (N.A.T.E.). This body's journal *English in Education* now commands a larger readership than the *Use of English*, and its concerns are more practical. It also shows a less prejudiced view of the relationship between literary and linguistic studies.

The influence of Leavis can be seen at its best, perhaps, in Frank Whitehead's *The Disappearing Dais* (Chatto and Windus, 1966). Here are all the familiar elements—the concern for tradition, for literature, for quality; the impatience with the linguistic study of language; and the elevated claims for the role of criticism in training the educated man. But there is also the healthy common-sense of an experienced practitioner. Limited somewhat by his largely selective school experience, Whitehead's book is remarkably free from elitism and remains one of the best of the many books on English teaching written in the post-war years.

A quite different book, written at much the same time, is Patrick Creber's *Sense and Sensitivity* (University of London Press, 1965), which was based firmly on experience in an urban comprehensive school. The author focuses on what children write, and how to guide them to write it. He shares Whitehead's practical experience, his good sense in the analysis of classroom events, and his impatience with English work which is merely pious convention. As an account of a genuinely comprehensive basis for English work it ultimately fails: the book's persistent labelling of pupils as belonging to academic and non-academic streams suggests that we have not yet achieved Sampson's common school. But although Whitehead and Creber could not yet achieve a synthesis which would meet the needs of English teaching over the whole secondary range, they both escaped from the sterile ideological squabbles of English teaching, and enabled the growing body of English specialists in non-selective schools to develop thought and practice on wider lines than *The Use of English* and its associated groups had been able to do.

Romantic Calvinism

David Holbrook's earliest books on English teaching were a liberating force. *English for Maturity* (C.U.P., 1961) and *English for the Rejected* (C.U.P., 1964) were attempts to work out the implications of Leavis' position for the teaching of the subject in schools. It may seem hard to believe this now, but Holbrook was in fact the first writer to become widely known, within the profession and beyond it, who took the teaching of English with second-ary modern children seriously. He was the first to say audibly in public that the subject might have more to offer than 'giving the basics' to less gifted children. In doing so, he brought an access of professional self-respect to hundreds of English teachers, and this strenuous moral support is still the basis of his influence. His books make many suggestions for classroom work, and his anthologies are likewise of practical value—although they were to be used extensively in selective schools quite as much as in the under-financed and under-esteemed secondary modern schools for which he designed them. Almost a whole generation of lecturers in colleges of education came to regard these two seminal books as the best guide for student teachers, and many of them do so to this day.

In attempting to assess Holbrook's influence, we feel certain doubts. We believe, for example, that an essential element in the making of a good English teacher is the experience of teaching on the full-time staff of a school for four or five years. In fact, relatively little of Holbrook's teaching of school-age pupils up to 1964 had been on a full-time basis, and his early books leave a question in our minds about the full-time teacher's capacity to sustain the intense interest in every pupil and the very active classroom role that he proposes. We wonder, too, whether an eager acceptance of pupils' confidences may not at times have a touch of naiveté about it, since what pupils write is bound to reflect what they understand their teacher to be interested in.

Holbrook is deeply committed to the educative power of literature as the central element of our cultural heritage, and to the principle that literature educates by influencing the feelings. This brought about the anthology-making which led, among other books, to *People and Diamonds* (1962), *Visions of Life* (1964) and *Iron, Honey, Gold* (1966, all C.U.P.). These form a revealing commentary on their editor's conception of literature as it may apply in schools. For a severely restricted cast of authors is drawn upon. In prose, there are D.H. Lawrence, Scott Fitzgerald, T.F. Powys, Hemingway, and some 'modern' autobiographical writers. The poetry collections are more varied, but scarcely more catholic in taste: we find Lawrence again, Emily Dickinson, Arthur Waley, John Clare, and

Edward Thomas. The concerns of this poetry, which Holbrook clearly regards as more important than the prose, are with the world of childhood or with the countryside. It is a world at once innocent and uncorrupted—the vision of life is romantic.

The adjustment of English teaching to meet the needs of the full range of ability in the period since 1960 has proceeded rapidly. In the light of this, the approach to classroom activity outlined in David Holbrook's early books now seems strikingly teacher-centred. The treatment of literature which is proposed appears as a mediation of it by the teacher, and there is an underlying implication that many pupils are unable to make any direct response of their own. Holbrook recognizes, indeed, that many pupils of less than average ability cannot directly grasp the power and subtlety of great writing. For such children, creative writing was the technique which enabled the teacher to work with them instead of against them, and it is probably true to say that many of Holbrook's followers in this regard have been unduly tolerant of technical inadequacy in the interest of preserving their pupils' creativity. The limitations of Holbrook's early work are seen particularly clearly in the list of children's fiction which he commends for use in schools in his textbook for college of education students: few of them were written after 1920 and most need interpretation by an actively dominant teacher. However, it is necessary to qualify these strictures, for in his most recent work on English teaching, Holbrook's approach seems to have undergone a change. In *English in Australia Now* (C.U.P., 1973) there is a great deal with which we would warmly agree, especially about the impossibility of conducting a humane curriculum in utterly inhumane settings.

Holbrook's major contribution has been in giving legitimacy to imaginative writing as a classroom activity for pupils of all levels of age and ability. His advocacy led many teachers to discover its possibilities who would not otherwise have done so. One may wonder whether any purpose is served by calling it 'creative', when all novice writing must be derivative in some degree and so much of it depends on the stimuli provided by the teacher. But imaginative writing is the expressive counterpart to the exploration of the world of feeling which literature alone can bring to the curriculum. Not all teachers would accept Holbrook's own account of its purposes:

> The child, in an atmosphere of trust, encouragement, and sympathy, can bring out inward torments in symbolic form . . . . In school he may obtain relief, satisfaction—and literacy.

Imaginative writing is here viewed as a therapy, and much of Holbrook's later writing is preoccupied with the symbolic significance of such expression. This is an aspect of his work into which relatively few teachers have followed him, but he has attempted to meet his critics' view and to dissociate himself from some of his more dubious adherents. For many teachers, the classroom which became as much of an emotional hothouse as the words just quoted suggest would be seen as rather unhealthy, and possibly as infringing the privacy of the pupil. But the second claim, that imaginative writing directly fosters literacy, can only be true in the lay sense of 'literacy', meaning 'ability to write correct English'. Nevertheless, Holbrook's emphasis on the need for motivation in pupils' writing commands very wide agreement. He has now lent his support, also, to the use of good contemporary children's fiction in schools, and *English in Australia Now* includes a longer list than we have space for.

In many of his writings, Holbrook evinces a Rousseau-like belief in the innocence of childhood. This romanticism underpins and provides the inner energy for his strong and deep concern with English teaching. It carries with it, however, a view of adolescents and adults as only too corruptible, and latent in his romanticism is a strongly Calvinist streak which has emerged in his strident attacks on pornography. His advocacy of censorship seems fundamentally authoritarian and even alarmist, seeking to sweep away whatever does not accord with its own view of moral worth. Some would think such a position implies an admission of defeat for English teaching and all it stands for.

An associated figure is Fred Inglis. In his *The Englishness of English Teaching* (Longman, 1969) there is a sub-stratum of factual inquiry into school English syllabuses. But the book opens with a telling quotation from Stephen Marshall, who preached in 1641: ' . . . you have great works to do, the planting of a new heaven and a new earth among us, and great works have great enemies.' The 'great enemies' are the same as ever, now drearily predictable: the manipulators of language, the hard-nosed intellectuals, and the purveyors of the popular culture of the masses. But there is no really adequate analysis of how this culture operates or of the linguistic patterns of its usage. And the book builds up to the ritual paean to the Baptist of the new movement:

> However Calvinist it sounds, I am asking for a militancy against all that is hateful in contemporaneity, and for a brave access of energy to build on those things we have which are worth holding. If we bend to the pressures, we become stool-pigeons and we abandon our Englishness and our seriousness; as has been finely said in an analogous context, we

have a world to win. It is Leavis who has made the essential definitions
for us; he, supremely, has given style and direction to our notions of
Englishness, culture, intelligence and sensibility, and to the stance for
combat . . . . (p. 187)

The echoes of Cromwell here are very strong: the day of Armageddon is at
hand. No other party, no other view, is allowed moral credit or legitimate
dissent. Such definitions are not so much essential as deeply prejudicial to
serious debate. They embody a pride which has marked too many reformers
in the world of English teaching. Their only redeeming feature is that the
excess and zeal of their comprehensive rejection of the contemporary are
self-defeating.

The relationship between school and community can be viewed, it is
true, as a battle-ground for the soul of English civilization. But to suggest
that it is a battle which the schools can win is to misconceive its terms. To
suggest further that English teachers can or should fight this holy war on
the basis that every other educational or cultural agency is in 'enemy' hands
is the veriest absurdity, and in our experience is ultimately subversive of
what it sets out to defend. It is particularly sad that all this should be
represented as the gospel of a great university teacher who never ventured
to set himself up as an authority on English teaching in secondary schools.
There were gaps and blindnesses in the work of Leavis, some of which have
cost him worldly and professional rewards commensurate with his influence,
but Inglis' kind of hagiography is fundamentally unfair. It confines and
reduces Leavis to the stature of a querulous and jaundiced Canute. We
would think the serious student likely to find surer guidance in Sampson,
Caldwell Cook, and Leavis himself: they maintain moral priorities,
without reducing their position to a mere 'stance for combat'.

Dartmouth and after

The American counterpart of N.A.T.E. initiated a specialist conference
which met for a full month in 1966 at Dartmouth College in the U.S. The
intention was to make a contribution to English teaching analogous to
that of the Woods Hole Conference in science teaching—a venture which
has by no means fulfilled the intentions of its participants. The forty-odd
delegates included many university professors of English from the U.S., who
represented a bewildering variety of schools of linguistics. The British con-
tingent, largely chosen by N.A.T.E., was naturally weighted towards teachers
in the Leavis tradition, and included among others Whitehead, Holbrook,
and Boris Ford. But it also included other, more eclectic individuals.
Nothing could have been more ill-assorted than the assumptions which the

participants brought to Dartmouth, but the month-long seminar left very few views untouched. Each side commissioned a participant to write a book about it, and the English account, John Dixon's *Growth Through English* (O.U.P., 1966), broke away from all established positions to propose a new model.

Dixon's model focused on 'personal growth':

> Language is learned in operation, not by dummy runs. In English, pupils meet to share their encounters with life, and to do this effectively they move freely between dialogue and monologue—between talk, drama, and writing: and literature, by bringing new voices into the classroom, adds to the store of shared experience. Each pupil takes from the store what he can and what he needs. In doing so, he learns to use language to build his own representational world, and works to make this fit reality as he experiences it . . . In ordering and composing situations that in some way symbolise life as we know it, we bring order and composure to our inner selves. (p.13)

This passage is typical of Dixon's book, not least in its very tentative tone and its sense of wrestling with difficulties in the absence of an unquestioned ideology: the search is still going on. Dixon produced a remarkable synthesis of the variety of views current at the Dartmouth Seminar, and his 'growth' model has become influential among specialists. As we have suggested earlier, however, such a model contains an implicit analogy with biological growth which may be misleading. The book also rests on a largely personal or psychological view of the pupil's 'needs' which may undervalue his very practical need for the competence to survive in an advanced and literate society. But there is a striking absence of the well-established antithesis between literature and language, even though the real implications of the linguistic study language of English teaching remain to be worked out.

American experience of linguistic approaches had been far from encouraging. Chomsky's transformational grammar had been converted into schoolroom textbooks more immediately and assiduously than Leavis' emphasis on the close analysis of literary texts, but the effects on the pupil's writing competence were not obvious. The British response was less mechanistic and less dogmatic. Starting with a great emphasis on the role of talk, Andrew Wilkinson popularized the notion of 'oracy' (on the analogy of literacy and numeracy), and his *Foundations of Language* (O.U.P, 1971) is one of the most lucid accounts of the bearing of linguistic studies on all aspects of English teaching, including learning to read. The Schools Council financed a programme at University College, London, under Professor M.A.K. Halliday, in which one of the authors of this book participated, and the group which became the Language in Use Project set its face against

any attempt to programme the pupil's study of language. *Language in Use*
(Edward Arnold, 1972) is a substantial collection of guides to teaching
activities, which systematically invite the pupil, usually but not exclusively
in the middle and upper years of the secondary school, not to analyse
language but to explore it. The authors, P. Doughty, J. Pearce, and
G. Thornton, make their approach to language more explicit in *Exploring
Language* (Edward Arnold, 1972), a handbook for teachers which offers a
well-informed exposition of a very wide range of technical research in
readily comprehensible form. The emphasis of the *Language in Use*
materials is strongly towards a recognition of language as a social phenomenon, and towards an acknowledgement of the great diversity of written
and spoken English.

In addition to the experience of the Dartmouth Seminar, John Dixon's
work drew much sustenance from the work of James Britton and his
colleagues at the London Institute of Education. The magnitude of this
work, as a sustained intellectual enterprise, did not become apparent until
the publication of Britton's *Language and Learning* (Allen Lane, The Penguin
Press) in 1970. One of the most civilized and intelligent books ever written
about English teaching, this ranges widely in psychology, sociology, and
philosophy, and brings strengths from all these fields to bear on a series of
close studies of actual classroom behaviour. Britton has probably been the
most influential trainer of prospective teachers of English in this country
for many years. A number of his former students and colleagues have
gone on to make distinguished contributions of their own. Among these,
we should mention Douglas Barnes, who has become the leading British
exponent of the study of how teachers behave in classrooms. His initial
study, published in 1969 in *Language, the Learner, and the School*
(Penguin), has been influential out of all proportion to its length.

Many readers will be surprised that our account of the significant influences in English teaching in the last half-century makes no mention of
Bernstein and his concepts of restricted and elaborated codes. This work is
very technical research which has been almost universally misunderstood,
particularly by lecturers in colleges of education. Bernstein's codes are *not*
dialects. They are *not* ways of speaking. In this usage a 'code' is a mental
system, created by our early social experience, which leads us to organize
our behaviour, perceive reality, and explore, or reject, new meanings and
experience. It is a total misunderstanding of Bernstein to refer to a child
as 'speaking in restricted code'. We would regard any attempt to make
sense of Bernstein's research to students who have not pursued a serious
course in theoretical sociology as positively dangerous, because it is so likely

to leave behind the impression, which many teachers now have, that restrictedness of code is a permanent condition of the mind rather than the product of a social conditioning which may never be more than partial. To say this, of course, is not in any way to discredit Bernstein's own work. But the seriousness of the misunderstanding of Bernstein's work does point to the intense awareness that British people have about social class and social dialect: very abstract research which bears only indirectly on the topic has been made to sustain educational policies designed to reduce the apparent handicap of being born into the poorest strata of society.[1]

The present

Textbooks for English

Our brief review of some of the influences and shifts in the ideology of English teaching has concerned itself with the forces that give rise to textbooks rather than with the books themselves. Of the widely used English textbooks of the last thirty years, four call for mention. Ronald Ridout's *English Today* (Ginn & Co.) appeared in the 1940s and was a huge commercial success. From the point of view taken in this book it soon became an educational disaster. Raymond O'Malley and Denys Thompson's course *English One* to *English Five* (Heinemann, beginning 1955) has been a staple course book in grammar schools, and is probably the best example of the kind of course book which embodies traditional English teaching. If there has to be this fragmenting treatment of English, this example is lucid and reasonably humane, but both the authors would probably now wish it superseded. Much later, in 1963, John Dixon and two of his teaching colleagues in a London comprehensive published *Reflections* (O.U.P, 1963), an attempt to cater seriously for pupils over the whole range of ability. It was an instant success, and has had many imitators. Its limitations are now clear: snippets of literature are used to illustrate social arguments rather than as sources of literary insight or excitement, and the emphasis on 'discussion' without any very clear understanding of exactly what that meant laid ominous traps for the unwary. Among its descendants must rank the *Humanities Curriculum Project* (Heinemann), which seeks to engage pupils in schematic social studies on a basis of written material collected without adequate regard for its linguistic difficulty and with no serious interest in literary merit.

Some schools, and not a few engaged in training teachers, appear to believe that thorough-going use of the *Humanities Curriculum Project* can fully discharge a school's responsibilities for teaching English. We have suggested at a number of points in other chapters that the subject-matter of English cannot properly exclude what the jargon calls 'the affective domain'—the world of feeling, emotion, and attitude. Advocates of the Humanities material would argue that it caters very fully for attitudes and their modification. That it caters for the world of feeling adequately we would dispute. The Humanities Project's supporters would not claim, of course, to be concerned in any direct way with the area of competence in the use of language. The reliance of the project on group discussion of a special kind, which, in our view, needs more systematic training of the teacher than it usually receives, certainly contributes to the building of language competence, but this is fortuitous rather than planned. Any other aspect of language learning, under the umbrella of the Project, will be even more accidental.

The fourth body of classroom material published commercially to call for serious attention is probably the most distinguished of the four, but it is a series rather than a single book. The *Penguin English Project* contains a wide range of anthologies, printed with little or no commentary or question matter, prepared by practising teachers on a variety of themes. The books are exceptionally well printed and illustrated, and while they vary in quality the general level is astonishingly high. The school which has no specialist in English but wants to do justice to the work could do much worse than base its approach on a judicious selection of these anthologies and careful attention to the Teachers' Books.

English, language, and the school
The teacher, as the one adult user of language in the room, is a figure whose importance we have stressed many times in these pages. The headmaster who wanted his pupils to learn how to talk easily to headmasters reminds us that this language-using role of the teacher is by no means peculiar to English teachers. Every teacher, whether returning history essays, announcing the games results at assembly, turning the pupils out of the classroom at break, or explaining with a note of urgency that a phosphorus solution left to dry in a plastic sink will burn down the lab—each of these is part of the school as a language environment. That environment, just because it is different from the home and commands some measure of prestige in the eyes of many of the pupils, is a source of language models to the children in the school. We have mentioned in this paragraph a set of very varied social settings for language, and the language that ensues is distinctive in each setting. Indeed, to use language peculiar to one setting in a quite different one is a staple of comedians. Pupils in schools learn much more than the school consciously

sets out to teach them, and of all these elements in the 'hidden curriculum' the diverse ways of using language are among the most potent.

The teacher who shouts at his pupils is, among other things, teaching shouting—and some pupils acquire this instrumental model of language only too well. If talk is important in the overt curriculum, it is just as important in the hidden one. This has all sorts of implications. In the 9 to 13 age range it almost certainly points to dining arrangements involving small tables and outdoor play areas which provide sheltered spaces for talk as well as open expanses for energetic games. Again, if the role of adults as speakers of English matters, so does their role as listeners, and this is seriously impeded if the main relationship between teachers and pupils is one of fear. Very similar considerations apply to the written communication between school and pupil. The headmistress who insisted that all duplicating of material for class use should be typed by the school secretary had this much point, that there would be no more marginless masses of uneven type laid before the pupils, and the things that the teachers said about presentation would at least be matched by what they were seen to do about it. Again, the way in which a school formulates its rules can distance the pupils by using the passive voice, or it can engage their cooperation. This was put firmly into practice by the middle school headmaster in the north of England who sent to every pupil before he entered the school a letter which went like this:

> You have been to our school on a visit and have a good idea of the sort of school it is. We don't have many rules, though we do have some likes and dislikes that you will soon pick up from your class teachers. There are two do's and two don'ts:
> do enjoy school   do tell us if something's wrong
> don't spit   and   don't smell.

Some of the parents objected, but the children did have baths!

Beyond the role of the school as a language-using community is the role of the individual members of the teaching staff and their responsibility for spoken and written language in all parts of the curriculum. We began the Preface with a reference to the oft-quoted adage about every teacher being a teacher of English. We are led to end this book with a renewed emphasis on the fact that because all subjects of the curriculum are conducted in English they are also in some measure teaching English. This is not a mere quirk of the authors: it has become, in recent years, a central preoccupation of leading specialists in English teaching. We have pointed out already the unrealistic expectations of teachers who never correct mis-spellings in pupils' work in their own subjects, but are outspoken in the staffroom about how English teachers are falling down on the job. Children who 'are not taught to spell nowadays' are being 'not taught' by a majority of their teachers. This is a battle the English teacher cannot hope to win on his own. On the other hand, for a staff collectively to decide to 'have a blitz on spelling' is probably worse than useless. Rather, what is needed is a continuous self-training by a school's staff, giving rise to discussion of a common policy about language involving such things as methods of marking, the use of classroom talk, the role of dictated notes and reference books.

As Douglas Barnes has shown, the staff's own use of language in the classroom is a vital part of the school's language climate. Self-inspection of the kind suggested by Barnes' use of tape-recorded lessons is a demanding exercise, and while it can be shocking at first it is remarkable in its effects. Of all the possible activities for the massive expansion of in-service training promised in the next few years, none seems to us more important than this. A school policy about language does not simply happen: it has to be brought about by a sensitive and growing concern.

The status of English
Many teachers, including many English specialists, are increasingly uncertain at the present time about what their subject comprises. We have shown how, during the present century, one inadequate model of English after another has held sway and given place. Now, with the vogue for 'language across the curriculum' (see Douglas Barnes *et al, Language, the Learner, and the School,* Penguin, especially Part III) on the one hand, and for integration on the other, one may reasonably wonder what is the place of the English teacher. In some schools, indeed, English as a 'subject' has disappeared, swallowed up in the voracious maw of the 'integrated day' of some junior schools or of the 'humanities' at the secondary level. Where the integration produces elements entitled 'communications', or work-schemes mention 'the English skills' with a becoming piety, one may wonder whether anything of significance is left. In many cases the product of this integration is indeed greater than the sum of its parts: Tom Haggitt's *Working with Language* (Blackwell, 1967) shows how a large group of children from an urban school could descend on a Worcestershire village and spend a week there learning about the village as a whole. It is a valuable and convincing demonstration. But as the book's title suggests, the teacher who made it had language itself as one of his priorities. Where this is not so, some things may be lost unless they are specifically built into the work, and English is perhaps more at risk in this way than most other elements in the curriculum.

For many children English is the only element in the curriculum where they have been encouraged to explore and express their own feelings, and to come to terms with them through story and poetry. It is also the only one where the choice of story and poetry and play is directed towards enabling children to explore the feelings and experiences of others and to respond to them imaginatively. If these aspects of English are allowed to slip through the net of integrated humanities projects, our pupils will pay a fearful price in due time. For such an oversight allows English to become a 'service subject' providing the language skills which other subjects demand, and in the real, competitive world of education a service subject loses status and resources. A 'service' basis for English has proved a disaster in further education, and would just as surely do likewise in schools. In many cases, however, this destruction of the integrity of English is more likely to take the form of calling the English component of an integrated curriculum 'English skills'. Such a nomenclature opens the door to a systematic re-duction of the time available for English, and for a steady dilution of the quality and training of the teachers deputed to teach it. Even when the 'English skills' approach is well done, it is not enough. We have seen many junior school classrooms where the children write a great deal, and where presentation and mechanical accuracy reach high standards—but where almost all that is written is in reality copied from books of reference. The inhumanity, the illiberalism, of this conception of English is destructive of much that is most to be treasured in childhood. It may not need an English specialist to preserve in a school the scope for imagination, invention, fantasy, and the poetic, but it does need someone who cares about these things.

In the same way, the junior schools of many education authorities in England are well supplied with books of reference and reading schemes and 'extension readers', but because nobody has become concerned about imaginative literature they are bare of good children's fiction and have only the most rudimentary resources of poetry. To remedy this does not require an English specialist, once again, but needs a teacher who cares. This simple need for concern extends to headteachers, too, of course. A random sample of a hundred posts of seniority advertised for junior schools while this book was being written revealed that only one in ten mentioned English or language development, while forty asked applicants to take responsibility for mathematics, and many of the rest appeared to be looking, quite simply, for men. English in the junior school is still, to an extent, in need of the kind of support which the Newbolt Report gave to it in secondary schools.

Where next?

We have written this book with a concern to help the non-specialist teacher of English. It has been able to do little more than scratch the surface of the more fundamental questions facing the specialist branch of the profession, but we hope we have sketched out an approach which at least makes initial sense. Teachers who attempt to carry it into practice must expect to feel isolated and troubled over many details. We have urged the importance of discussion in the learning of pupils, and would urge it in the learning of teachers also. The great majority of teachers' centres, and most courses of in-service training, offer opportunities for just such discussion of teachers' problems. One of the problems for this area of English teaching is precisely that most courses are set up for specialists, but wardens of teachers' centres usually respond to an identifiable demand for particular patterns of in-service training. It is also quite mistaken to suppose that courses designed for specialist English teachers are likely to be unwelcoming to the newcomer who wants to learn about the job.

There are three particular channels which we want to mention in this context. A number of research and development projects have been set up by the Schools Council and other bodies in the field of English teaching. In several cases, the belief of practising specialists in relying on 'coalface' experience has meant that projects have been based largely or entirely on building up networks of contact with other practising teachers. These networks have been by no means confined to specialists. Information about such projects is published regularly in *Dialogue*, the Schools Council's termly journal, or can be obtained from the Information Office, Schools Council, 160 Great Portland Street, London W1N 6LL.

Secondly, we would mention the role of the L.E.A. English adviser. We may be taking a rosy view of his function, since both of us have served in it, but the English Adviser's job is both to get into a wide variety of schools and to be professionally up to date about his subject. We can say quite confidently that the great majority of advisers now in service will be sympathetic to the approaches to English teaching outlined in this book. The proportion of Education Authorities with specialist English advisers is growing steadily. A teacher wanting to put some of our suggestions into practice and facing either practical difficulties or a need for discussion will normally find his L.E.A. adviser a useful person to turn to.

Thirdly, the National Association for the Teaching of English, which we have mentioned earlier in this chapter, provides a wide range of services to members. These include the use of an Advisory Officer who will answer by post many queries about English teaching; a termly journal which prints a wide variety of articles and always includes some offering practical advice; and the annual conference at which some 400 English teachers from primary schools to universities assemble to discuss common concerns. The Association has branches throughout the country which enable members to maintain informal contact or to operate in working parties and study groups. (Hon. Secretary, 5 Imperial Road, Edgerton, Huddersfield, HD3 3AF.)

The exploration of English teaching in this book is only a beginning, and we have sought to conduct it on the basis that most of our readers will want to take some aspect of it further. We have tried to be brief, and in doing so have left questions unanswered, but if we have been of practical use to a baffled or apprehensive teacher, we shall have served our turn.

Sources and resources I

The aim of this section is to give information to the hard-pressed teacher about obtaining the materials he may need. It also seeks to highlight the role of resources in teaching, and is arranged in sections which correspond to a natural layout of resource centres. Printed materials come first; non-print materials cover audio, visual, and audio-visual resources in that order; there is a section about equipment; and a closing note on libraries.

Most teaching in the past relied on the resources of textbook and teacher's talk and chalk. Anything beyond this was illustrative or additional, and related directly to what the teacher had to say. The present position is different: in order to organize situations in which diverse pupils can learn, much more is needed. The problems of keeping the new resources under control are discussed in detail in *School Resource Centres* (Schools Council Working Paper 43, Evans/Methuen). This defines a 'resource' as 'anything which may be an object of study or stimulus for the pupil'. Its list of examples goes on: 'books, periodicals, newspapers, press cuttings, pictures, diagrams, maps, charts, photocopies and microforms, worksheets, slides, film-strips, film-loops, records, audio-tapes, radio and television programmes, video-tapes, slide/tape and filmstrip/record combinations, multi-media kits, programmed materials, models, specimens and realia, as well as individuals and objects in the community.' The paper sets out examples of the best current practice for full-scale resource centres, but in most cases the teacher for whom this book is written will have to build his own smaller bank of material. In doing this, he should grasp the difference between using resources to supplement his own teaching, and using resources as direct learning-material for the pupil. Since the latter approach is implicit in much else in this book, and calls for more extensive materials of all kinds, our account of these refers at many points to materials which need no teacher to mediate them to the pupil. The diversity and range of materials necessary for this more pupil-centred approach will also be useful to the teacher who is free to work in a more traditional way. (See L.C. Taylor, *Resources for Learning*, Penguin.)

Print materials

Books

In addition to the books used in specific parts of English class work, every English teacher needs in his classroom two basic collections:
1. A classroom library of fiction related to the age and interests of the pupils.
2. A collection of simple reference books.

1. *Children's fiction.* Far too few English teachers have read enough children's literature, and there is much too limited a recognition of the achievements in this field in the last twenty years. Sources and Resources II lists some books which we have found very widely liked by children aged 9 to 13 and which give them a much sounder basis for later studies of literature than the so-called classics. But the classroom library will need many more books, and while Puffin Books are not the only reputable publishers of novels for children their list has an enduring distinction. Other lists worth consulting are Brockhampton Press, for its Black Knight range; Macmillan (Club 75 and Topliners), Heinemann (New Windmill Library, covering a wider age range), O.U.P. (for its children's paperbacks), and Collins (Armada Lion, reprints of many titles formerly in the Puffin series). Most of these are paperbacks, and the very high standards of print and design set by Puffin Books have been widely maintained.

A second category of children's fiction, especially for children of 9 and 10, is the large, well-illustrated book of well-known or collected stories. Oxford University Press, Methuen, Dent, Odhams, and Brockhampton are among the most successful in this area, meeting the real need for clearly printed versions of stories which many children of this age already know but may not have met in writing. The teacher should look for these in the library catalogue issued by each publisher, not the textbook list.

A considerable literature has grown up about children's reading, but no first-rate literary critic has yet accorded the genre the serious critical attention it deserves. By far the widest and most detailed bibliography available is Margery Fisher's *Intent upon Reading* (Brockhampton, 1969). A valuable supplementary source is the termly journal *Children's Literature in Education* (Ward Lock). Of the remainder, Aidan Chambers' *The Reluctant Reader* (Pergamon, 1969) gives a lively if sardonic view of some school libraries and their failings, and is perceptive about why some children do not enjoy books. Dan Fader, in *Hooked on Books* (Pergamon, 1969), makes a convincing case that for deprived children, at least initially, quantity matters more than quality. The main sources of middle-of-the-road comment and selections are the School Library Association (Premier House, 150 Southampton Row, London WC1B 5AR), which has a subscription scheme of great value to the school librarian, and the National Book League (7 Albemarle Street, London W1X 4BB).

2. *A basic reference library.* Useful reference books *for teachers* are mentioned throughout this book. Here we would add

> Brewer's *Dictionary of Phrase and Fable* (Cassell)
> *Concise Oxford Dictionary*
> Larousse *Encyclopaedia of Mythology* (Hamlyn)
> G. Palmer and N. Lloyd, *A Year of Festivals* (Warne)
> Penguin *Dictionary of Modern Quotations*
> Penguin *Dictionary of Quotations*
> Roget's *Thesaurus of English Words and Phrases* (Penguin)

There are many thousands of reference books for children, and each classroom needs a selection related to the prospective users. We think it is a fallacy to suppose that children under the age of 13 have much use for a major encyclopaedia such as the Britannica. Even a Children's Britannica is only as useful as the child's grasp of its indexing and arrangement. Rather, teachers might consider such series as the following:

> The Oxford Children's Reference Library
> MacDonald's Junior Reference Library
> The Observer Books (Warne)
> Hamlyn's All-colour Paperbacks
> The How and Why Wonder Books (Transworld)
> The Oxford Junior Encyclopaedia

In this connection it is much more useful to have a classroom poetry shelf than to buy class sets of a single book. These are some of the more useful for this age range:

> M.G. and P. Benton, *Touchstones* I and II (U.L.P.)
> Edward Blishen, *Oxford Book of Poetry for Children*
> C. Copeman and J. Gibson, *As Large as Alone* (Macmillan)
> E. Graham, *Puffin Quartet of Poets* (Penguin)
> Raymond O'Malley and Denys Thompson, *The Key of the Kingdom* (Chatto and Windus)
> James Reeves, *Merry-Go-Round* (Heinemann)
> A.F. Scott, *Poems for Pleasure* I (C.U.P.)

Geoffrey Summerfield, *Junior Voices* and *Voices One* (Penguin)
M. Wollman and D. Grugeon, *Happenings* I (Harrap)
M. Wollman and A.L. Austin, *Happenings* II (Harrap)

Closely related to the poetry shelf are Poemcards (Harrap) and Poetry
Cards (Macmillan), and the single sheets issued to go in folders that develop
into pupils' individual anthologies: the sheets of poems can be bought
singly or in class sets from a wide range. Specimen sets from White Rose
Educational Resources, 32 Roe Lane, Southport, Lancs., PR9 9EA, which
publish on behalf of the English Speaking Board.

Other printed material
Comprehensive and almost indispensible is T.G. Jeremiah's *Source Book of
Creative Themes* (Blackwell, 1972), an index of material and resources for
some eighty themes, listing stories, books, poems, records, films, charts, and
much else in a way which will save many teachers long hours of searching.
As it is only an index, its listings need evaluating by the user in the light of
his particular purpose.

A general guide to non-print resources which is practical and kept up-to-
date is the *Treasure Chest for Teachers* (Schoolmaster Publ. Co., for the
N.U.T.). This enables one to select wisely from the mass of commercial,
sponsored, and near-advertising material available in the form of charts,
booklets, and kits of specimens. It also indicates which business firms will
deal with requests from teachers only, and this preference should be strictly
adhered to, since too many requests from children may even lead firms to
close down their services to teachers. The same book lists the embassies and
public services which will provide free teaching material, some of it of high
quality. Here we should mention the Post Office, which has a range of
excellent materials on communications. Full details from Public Relations
Dept., The Post Office, St. Martin's-Le-Grand, London EC1A 1HQ.

More general chart and kit materials can be found in the catalogues of
Educational Productions Ltd., East Ardsley, Wakefield, Yorks., and
Pictorial Charts Educational Trust, 132–8 Uxbridge Road, West Ealing,
London W13. However, wall charts need care, because many of them
crowd in too much material. For guidance on this matter and on effective
display, consult R. Leggat—*Showing Off—Display Techniques for the Teacher*,
(Educational Foundation for Visual Aids, 33 Queen Anne St.,
London W1M OAL. The same body's catalogue of wall charts is also useful.)

There is a steady flow of kits of all kinds appearing in schools, many of
them developed by Schools Council Projects. As a broad rule of thumb,

materials in this form which focus on a curriculum subject should be used by or in close collaboration with a specialist, while more general kit materials in practice need a great deal of care and study before they can be made to work well in the classroom. One example, which happens to be mainly in printed form, is *Jackdaws* (Jonathan Cape): mostly on historical topics, these collections of documents are interesting to an academic type of pupil, but many of the papers are in very small print and their language can be very difficult.

Non-print materials

Audio-materials

These comprise records and tapes. In practice, discs are more useful to teachers and cassette tape-recordings are more useful to pupils. Cassettes can be stored and indexed easily, and readily accumulate to form a useful library. With machines that play back only there is no risk of erasing the recording by accident. Tape libraries should draw on a wide range of broadcasts, music, speech, and features (see also the E.F.V.A. catalogue of *Records and Tapes for Education*). Cassette tapes have gained some reputation for poor quality, especially of music, but this is now being overcome.

1. Some record labels deserve special mention:
    Argo Record Co. Ltd., 115 Fulham Road, London SW3. A Decca subsidiary; some materials now produced by Decca Educational Services. Good range of poetry and folk, especially some of the original Radio Ballads.
    Jupiter Recordings, 140 Kensington Church St., London W8. Many high-quality speech records, including poetry anthologies compiled for younger children with the text published in book form.
    Caedmon Records: John Murray Ltd., 65 Clerkenwell Road, London EC1. Many speech records, mainly of classic plays, but including readings of Lewis Carroll and Edward Lear.
    Topic records Ltd., 27 Nassington Road, London NW3. The major source of recorded folk-song; the catalogue, *Topics for Teachers*, lists by subject. Specially recommended are *Streets of Song* (Behan and MacColl, 12T41) and *English and Scottish Ballads* (Lloyd and MacColl, 12T103).
    B.B.C. Radio Enterprises, Villiers House, Haven Green, London W5. Has a short but growing list, mainly old broadcasts, but including the cheapest good-quality records of sound effects.

I.L.E.A. London Tape Library, All Souls Primary School, Foley St., London W1. Useful collections of tapes produced within I.L.E.A. and available on loan at low charges.

· 2.   Using records and tapes: the best non-technical guide is Graham Jones, *Teaching with Tape* (Focal Press). For more technical guidance the information in B.A.S.F.'s *Tape Questions—Tape Answers*, available free from the area B.A.S.F. representative, can be readily adapted to most other equipment.

Visual materials

The Educational Foundation for Visual Aids (E.F.V.A. address on p.142 above) is the standard source of information on all kinds of visual aids. Its sectional catalogue (Section 1 deals with English) is up-to-date and thorough. E.F.V.A. has recognized the menace of out-of-date catalogues and runs a scheme called VENISS: for an annual subscription of £3·50 the school can receive copies of all publications as they appear. English teachers will have use for the following main types of material and will build up collections of them.

1.   *Photographs*.   Flexible and cheap. Some published sets for English teachers (e.g. M. Marland, *Pictures for Writing*, Blackie; Esmor Jones, *Camera Explorations*, Pergamon) have their limitations and date easily. Better sources are large public libraries, photographs taken by teachers and pupils, and periodicals, especially the colour magazine supplements. (The *Daily Telegraph* usually has large stocks of back numbers of its colour supplement, supplied free to educational institutions; the two Sunday supplements also supply bulk orders but charge for them.) Most newspapers sell prints of pictures taken by staff photographers, and the *Guardian* is particularly helpful in this.

Photographs can be used for display, to illustrate pupil's work, to stimulate drama or writing, and to start off group discussion. Old snapshots from family albums are very useful in the last of these. Nearly all children of 13 can learn to operate a simple still camera, and those with reading and writing problems can do very good work with it, gaining a measure of success in an otherwise frustrating schooling.

2.   *Paintings*.   Large reproductions for classroom use are an under-used source of imaginative stimulus, and could be found more often on classroom walls. Most of the major galleries have catalogues of reproductions, and several commercial firms publish high-quality ones. T.G. Jeremiah, *op.cit.* pp.98—115, gives an indexed list of the most useful works and their sources.

3. *Slides and filmstrips*. For viewing by the whole class or, more especially, by small groups.

> (i) Galleries selling slides of items in their collections:
> National Gallery, Trafalgar Square, London WC2.
> National Gallery of Scotland, The Mound, Edinburgh 1.
> Wallace Collection, Manchester Square, London W1.
> British Museum, Bloomsbury, London WC1.
> (ii) Commercial slides and filmstrips. The best commercial source of slides is probably Woodmansterne Ltd., Watford Industrial Estate, Watford, Herts: a wide-ranging list, classified, of very high quality slides. Good sources of filmstrips include:
> Common Ground Ltd., Longman Group, Burnt Mill, Harlow, Essex.
> Diana Wyllie Ltd., 3 Park Rd., Baker St., London NW1 (also make storage systems for slides and slide/tape combinations).
> Visual Education Ltd., Hawkley Studios, Liss, Hampshire.
> This is a very small selection from a long list, given in full by Jeremiah (*op,cit.*, pp.157–8), and we do not imply that these three firms are necessarily better than their competitors.

4. *Film-loops*. The filmstrip is a set of stills on a single strip, and many teachers have become dubious of its value in the television age, since pupils quickly find it tedious. The filmloop is in effect a cassetted film which runs for about four minutes and repeats itself until the viewer is turned off. Very few have been made which are of any value to English teachers, but Nuffield science ones may be well worth borrowing.

Audio-visual materials

1. *Film-making*. The teacher skilled in film work brings to English teaching a very valuable asset, and an English department should regard film-making as a no less logical extension of its work than drama. It is a field in which unexpected gifts emerge in unlikely children, and which leads to a great deal of constructive talk. Nor is film-making anything like as costly or difficult as it might appear. Like drama, of course, it needs a secure base of good discipline, and it takes a good teacher to steer his class through the preparatory study of method to the final editing, but children of 12 and 13 have made rewarding films. A Super-8 vision-only camera is a quite feasible purchase for many schools, but many Teachers' Centres have loan equipment. Educationally the objectives of film-making should be to engage the pupils in a sustained corporate activity which sharpens their awareness of non-verbal communi-

cation and develops their powers of social co-operation. A good handbook is
D. Lowndes–*Film-making in Schools* (Batsford, 1968).

  · Whereas film has to be professionally developed and can be used only
once, videotape can be used many times over and can be played back
immediately. After its high initial cost it may well be more useful than
film. A very different medium from film, videotape can do most of the
things that film can do in schools, and it would be sad if the V.T.R. equipment now coming into more and more schools were confined to the off-
air recording of T.V. programmes. In particular the link with drama work
and the freedom to re-take a rehearsal or performance that videotape
provides has many unexplored possibilities, Here, as in other uses, the
decision to buy only one camera may be a false economy.

2.   *Using film*. Too long confined to the merely illustrative role of other
visual aids, or to courses in film-appreciation, film has many other uses
for English teaching. As a stimulus to talking and writing, as a communication medium in its own right, and as a means of interpreting and appreci-
ating literature, film has produced some masterpieces, and much of what
we have said about the study of literature applies to films as well. However,
many pupils' visual education is better than that of their teachers, and a
literary or analytic approach will strike them as condescending. The
response to visual media like film is not closely related to academic ability:
films are useful with *all* abilities.

  If the logical place for work on film in school is within the domain of
English, the same applies to television. Here we want to dissent from a
widespread practice among English teachers, whose chief 'use' of T.V. in
school is to illustrate 'mass media' courses designed to alert pupils to the
dangers of advertising and the like. We have found middle secondary pupils
just as aware of when they are being 'got at' as any adults, and indulgently
amused by teachers who show anxiety about this for their pupils, without
being aware of their own susceptibilities. The literary or moralistic stance
adopted from a blend of the Leavis tradition with the brash popularization of
Vance Packard cuts no ice with today's young, and is not relevant to
children under 13 anyway. It is far better to give them experience of the
good and sensitive cinematic work of art.

3.   *Sources*. For information and up-to-date help on all aspects of film in
education: Education Department, British Film Institute (B.F.I.), 81 Dean St.,
London W1V 6AA. The B.F.I.'s publications include:

B.F.I. Distribution Catalogue (50p). Lists the B.F.I.'s library, with much
historic material, and the B.F.I.'s other services.

B.F.I. Study Extract Catalogue. Detailed list of *extracts* from feature films: a
large and expanding collection, very useful for those on a limited budget.

Films on Offer. Summary of most 16mm. films available in this country.

Free B.F.I. publications include lists of current features, shorts, and
distributors; thematic materials, and teachers' accounts of work with
film. Write to the Teacher Adviser, Education Department, B.F.I.

The Society for Education in Film & Television (SEFT), 63 Old Compton
St., London W1V 5PN, runs a comprehensive information service for
members, and among several publications is its quarterly *Screen
Education Notes*. A more recently formed body, the National
Association for Film in Education, 3 The Croft, Wall Street,
London N1 3NB, issues a termly newsletter and is particularly
interested in the links between film and English teaching.

Short films, usually sponsored, can be obtained at low rentals from the
following, among many others:

British Transport Film Library, Melbury House, London NW1 6JU.

Canada House, Trafalgar Square, London SW1.

Canadian Travel Film Library, 1 Grosvenor Square, London W1.

Central Film Library, Govt. Buildings, Bromyard Avenue, London W37 JB.

Concord Films Ltd., Nacton, Ipswich, Suffolk IP1O OJZ.

Ford Film Library, 25 The Burroughs, London NW4.

National Coal Board Films, 68 Wardour St., London W1V 3HP.

Petroleum Films Bureau, 4 Brook St., London W17 1AY.

Scottish Central Film Library, 16—17 Woodside Terrace, Glasgow C3.

A film library on Standard 8 film is maintained by

Perry's Movies, 129 Kingston Road, London SW19,

and includes many feature films such as Hitchcock and Ford, shorts by
Chaplin, Laurel and Hardy, and others, at very low rentals.

Film catalogues are a useful addition to a staffroom library, but as we
have mentioned above some system of keeping them up to date is essential:
the lists change from year to year even more than do publishers' lists of
books, and in addition the distributors of particular films may change also.

4. *Broadcasts.* The many programmes available from the B.B.C. are of a
high technical standard, but they need using with care. They tend to be
broadcast in series, and the value of one such programme may depend on

a knowledge of others in the same series. Some of them are in fact more difficult for the pupil than they appear at first glance, especially in relation to the age range they claim to be for. Many of the readings of literature have an antiseptic quality unacceptable to many children, and like all other forms of oral communication need getting used to. For this reason the teacher will often find it useful to tape programmes, listen to them at leisure, and select or store them. However, the law of copyright governs all taped broadcasts, and a body which has rendered great service to education, as the BBC has done and continues to do, is entitled to its protection. Guidance about this matter is given in three pamphlets—

School Radio and the Tape Recorder
Using Radio & TV—a Guide to Classroom Practice
Videotape Recording and TV.

These are obtainable from The Schools Broadcasting Council for U.K., The Langham, Portland Place, London W1A 1AA. The same body can supply the address of the nearest BBC Education Officer, whose job is to advise schools on all aspects of using broadcasts. Such officers gladly visit schools for discussion, and provide both general and specialized in-service courses at Teachers' Centres.

The DES dealt with broadcasts in schools in one of its occasional *Reports on Education* (No.74, June 1972), which made a summary of a survey by H.M. Inspectors. It stressed that using broadcasts in schools is quite unlike using them in the home:

(i) To use a broadcast a teacher has to go to a little more trouble than is involved in a routine lesson. Undoubtedly the effort required in some schools is increased by a less than adequate supply of equipment, teachers' notes, and pupils' pamphlets. The great majority of schools visited in this survey were prepared to overcome these difficulties because of the improvement in the quality of education which could follow.
(ii) The effective use of broadcasting also calls for skill and understanding on the part of the teacher. The contribution made by broadcasting needs to be planned in relation to other resources available; broadcast material needs to be integrated into the work of the pupils; preparation is needed for actual broadcasts; the conditions under which broadcasts are received and used call for the exercise of particular teaching skills.

The pupils' pamphlets mentioned by the Report are available for most broadcasts, usually very well produced and modest in price. With or without the broadcasts they are good supplementary reading material. Those for the series *Listening and Writing* are a consistently good example. The growing body of broadcast-related material issued in recent years, although occasionally uneven in quality, is an important source for a school developing resources on a low budget. Apart from these pamphlets, tapes, filmstrips, and kits, many school T.V. programmes and sound broadcasts can be purchased on film or records. Catalogue from B.B.C. Radio & T.V. Enterprises, Villiers House, Ealing, London W5 2PA.

Equipment

This is not the place for technical detail, which can be obtained from the specialized reports published by the E.F.V.A. (address on p.142 above) and available under its VENISS scheme. These reports compare different makes dispassionately; and the equipment itself can be seen on display at the annual audio-visual exhibition called Inter-Navex, usually held at Olympia in July. The best current guide to educational use of equipment is R.P.A. Edwards, *Resources in Schools* (Evans, 1973). The journal *Visual Education* began in April 1972 to publish in serial form *A Teacher's AV Handbook*, intended for those with no practical experience in using such aids. Clear, detailed, and helpful, it is to be published in book form in 1974.

There is no uniform 'best' way to organize visual aids in a school: each school must find the pattern which fits the facilities of the building and the interests of the staff. However, there are two obvious categories of equipment in the context of this book, and we give an outline of them here to spell out assumptions on which the rest of the book is based.

Essential equipment
1. *Tape recorders*. One cassette recorder for each teaching space, and the scope to assemble five or six on occasion. At least one good heavy-duty spool-to-spool recorder, with which an extension speaker should be invariably used.

2. *Radio*. Unless a school is unusually efficient in its off-air recording, or a local Teachers' Centre records everything and stores the tapes for a month (as a few now do), an English department needs its own V.H.F. receiver, ideally as part of a radio-cassette-recorder which can be used for off-air recording while the teacher is working with a class. (Many teachers do not appear to realize the ease with which a spool tape can be transferred to a cassette and vice versa.)

3. *Reprographic equipment*. An English department has special needs here, and a teaching area set aside for the subject is not complete without a spirit duplicator and a copying machine. The latter may be flat-bed copier or (better) an infra-red one which can also make heat-copiers for the spirit duplicator and laminate single sheets: both copiers serve different purposes, but they and the spirit duplicator can be bought for under £150.

4. *Overhead projector*, reserved for departmental use or as standard equipment in every classroom.

5. *Audio-page or Synchrofax*: a versatile aid of great value in mixed-ability classes, especially when linked to an audio-distribution centre (which enables a group of pupils to listen to tape or disc without intrusion on others). See p.45.

6. *Two cassette-loading cameras such as the Instamatic.*

7. *Strip/slide viewers.*

8. *Record-players.*

These items need to be readily accessible to the English class, either as departmental stock, or as the bare minimum of school stock on which the English department has a recognized claim.

Highly desirable equipment

1. *Reprographic equipment*. Most schools have a stencil duplicator, but very few of them make anything like enough use of its capacity for multi-colour work. As many Local Authority visual-aids officers will confirm, an offset-litho installation is more economic than stencil-duplicating in most large secondary schools. All large schools should have an electronic stencil-cutter for making duplicator stencils from complex originals.

Much of this equipment is complex to use, and teachers are not paid their salaries to undertake clerical duties. Without training and the benefit of experience they can easily damage the machinery, and the ancillary and clerical staff can and should be trained accordingly.

2. *Film equipment.*
a) 16mm projector. A stop-mechanism to 'freeze' a frame is very desirable. Automatic-threading projectors may not yet be quite reliable enough, but expert opinion is divided.

b) Super-8 film camera and dual-standard projector (i.e. taking Standard-8 and Super-8).
c) One high-quality still camera (e.g. Praktika).

In all these categories it pays to go for quality, and local shopping-around is likely to be better than using a consortium supplier. Decide to spend as much as you can afford, and get sound advice, from several sources, on what to choose.

3. *TV equipment*. A middle school with eight classes should have at least two receivers. If V.T.R. facilities are added, two cameras are necessary if pupils are to do serious T.V. work, one of them a hand-held portable.

4. *Stereo record-player* of good quality, best combined with V.H.F. radio as part of the school's audio system.

5. *Strip/slide projector* for classroom use.

It is more important to have a limited stock of good A.V. equipment, and to keep it in good order, than to buy cheaply for quantity. Today's pupils can be very sophisticated about sound, and in any case an educational system which has long accepted the obligation not to be a visual desert should avoid being an acoustic slum.

Libraries in and out of school

A school library should above all be a place which makes children feel welcome. Shelves protected in wire netting or locked away from the pupils are an abomination. For detail about running a school library the most useful starting-point is R. Purton, *Surrounded by Books* (Ward Lock). Above all, the library should cater for the children's leisure interests: the hobbies section should always loom large, and the library should always provide a retreat from the playground: playground duty and library duty are two sides of one coin. The library needs to be open whenever it is possible, with attractive wall-displays, shows of children's work, and anything else which will contribute to the impression that books are a natural thing to use. Accordingly the library should not be hedged in with restrictions: silence rules are usually unenforceable and short-circuit the social training in consideration for others that a library can provide. The library should cover the normal school-subject areas, together with a wide range of fiction and leisure-reading. (It is a folly to classify some fiction as 'literature' and other novels as 'mere' fiction.) The stock should cater for a variety of reading levels without any attempt to mark out the books suitable for less skilled readers.

The Library Association (7 Ridgmount St., Store Street, London WC1E 7AE) in its guide *School Library Resource Centres* suggests minimum standards for stocking: in a primary school, not less than eight volumes per pupil; and not less than ten per pupil in middle and secondary schools. This pamphlet is full of ideas about planning and running school libraries. A school library must expect to lose between 2% and 4% of its stock each year, and a librarian who tolerates shoddy-looking stock is in reality encouraging his pupils to treat all the books badly. Librarians naturally want to see pupils instructed in the mysteries of the Dewey system of classifying library books, but we regard this as wasted effort with most pupils under 13. Pupils need to know the physical layout of a library rather than its classification system, and to be aware of how much a librarian can help them. A class of children aged 12 can, however, be taken into a library of reasonable size (say, 4,000 volumes) and asked to work out by observation and browsing how it is arranged. This kind of work helps to overcome the bewilderment that such a library can often create in young children. But the library should be every English teacher's commonest and readiest resource.

The same applies to public libraries. The organized visit to the local public library branch should appear in the work of every class of 10 year olds, and again at a later stage: pupils need to be shown where it is, how to join it, and how to make use of the librarian. Every English teacher should be in contact with the school library service of his own education authority and become aware of the range of services it can offer. Children's librarians are usually expert, not only in display and arrangement, but also in some particular field of children's books. Teachers, for their part, have a direct access to children's responses to books that specialist librarians are eager to secure. Closer contact between the two is likely to surprise the teacher about other facilities offered by public libraries—block loans of books, museum collections, and in many cases libraries of records or photographs or archives. Children's librarians are also apt to be expert in children's fiction, which they often order, not on the basis of the publishers' lists but on the basis of their own reading. They are frequently very gifted at reading to children, and welcome the chance to receive a class, show them the library, read them some samples, and supplement the work of every English teacher in a unique and invaluable way.

Sources and resources II

These books have been welcomed as enjoyable reading by many different kinds of children. The first group will appeal to the younger, the second to the older part of the 9 to 13 age range. The publisher of the paperback edition is given.

Prudence Andrew	*Ginger over the Wall*	Puffin
Nina Bawden	*A Handful of Thieves*	Puffin
John Christopher	*The White Mountains*	Black Knight
Elizabeth Enright	*The Four-Storey Mistake*	Puffin
Eleanor Graham	*The Children who Lived in a Barn*	Puffin
Rene Guillot	*Sirga*	Oxford
Ted Hughes	*The Iron Man*	Faber
Norman Hunter	*Incredible Adventures of Prof. Branestawm*	Puffin
Clive King	*Stig of the Dump*	Puffin
Astrid Lindgren	*Pippi Longstocking*	Oxford
L.M.Montgomery	*Anne of Green Gables*	Peacock
Bill Naughton	*The Goalkeeper's Revenge*	Puffin
E.Nesbit	*The Railway Children*	Puffin
Mary Norton	*The Borrowers*	Puffin
Philippa Pearce	*Tom's Midnight Garden*	Oxford
Gerald Raftery	*Snow Cloud, Stallion*	Puffin
Dodie Smith	*The Hundred and One Dalmatians*	Puffin
P.L.Travers	*Mary Poppins*	Armada Lion
Edith Unnerstad	*The Saucepan Journey*	Puffin
E.B.White	*Charlotte's Web*	Puffin

Richard Adams	*Watership Down*	Puffin
Richard Church	*The Cave*	Puffin
Eilis Dillon	*The Lost Island*	Faber
Gerald Durrell	*The New Noah*	Puffin
Leon Garfield	*Black Jack* (or *Mister Corbett's Ghost*)	Puffin
Alan Garner	*The Owl Service*	Peacock
John Gordon	*The Giant under the Snow*	Puffin
Alfred Hitchcock	*Ghostly Gallery*	Puffin
C.Walter Hodges	*The Namesake*	Puffin
Ann Holm	*I am David*	Puffin
Clive King	*The Twenty-two Letters*	Puffin
Madeleine L'Engle	*A Wrinkle in Time*	Puffin
James Vance Marshall	*Walkabout*	Peacock
Jack Schaefer	*Shane and other Stories*	Peacock
Ian Serraillier	*The Silver Sword*	Puffin
Rosemary Sutcliff	*Eagle of the Ninth*	Oxford
John Rowe Townsend	*Gumble's Yard*	Puffin
Ruth M.Underhill	*Antelope Singer*	Puffin
Jill Paton Walsh	*The Dolphin Crossing*	Puffin
T.H.White	*The Sword in the Stone*	Armada Lion

Notes

Chapter 1

1   The effect of large scale on the G.C.E. system is fully explored in J. Pearce, *School Examinations* (Collier-Macmillan).

2   For a vivid account of how teachers can become unduly attached to the form rather than the substance of the language of their pupils, see J.W.P. Creber, *Lost for Words* (Penguin), Chapter 1.

3   These questions are lucidly explored in Randolph Quirk, *The Use of English* (2nd edn., Longman), especially Supplement II.

4   Such as J. Watts, *Interplay* (Longman), a multi-media approach, in which the various elements are of rather uneven quality, but of strong appeal to children of 11 to 12. Nancy Martin's Oxford English Source Books, *Here, Now, and Beyond, Truth to tell,* and *Half-Way,* contain exhilarating material, and questions which have been well conceived for the more able or mature middle school pupil. An English course book for average pupils of this age, or suitable for mixed-ability classes, has been eagerly sought by publishers, but no-one has yet produced one which we would endorse as warmly. The truth may well be that such a prescription cannot be dispensed.

Chapter 2

1   This topic is a major preoccupation of scholars in educational philosophy and educational sociology. See, for example, Richard Hooper (ed.) *The Curriculum: context, design, and development* (Oliver and Boyd for the Open University).

Chapter 3

1   'The integrated day' is now a widely current term for infant and junior school practice, where the conventional timetable is abandoned. The work of each group of pupils is planned in such a way that all the elements of the curriculum are dealt with, although the activities of the children may be hard to classify under particular 'subjects'. See, for example, Jack Walton (ed.), *The Integrated Day in Theory and Practice* (Ward Lock), and M. Brown and N. Precious, *The Integrated Day in the Primary School* (Ward Lock).

2   John Masefield, 'Reynard the Fox' in *Dauber and Reynard the Fox*, (Heinemann); Henry Williamson, *Tarka the Otter* (Puffin); Ted Hughes, 'Esther's Tomcat' in *Penguin Book of Animal Verse*; Philippa Pearce, *A Dog so Small* (Puffin); Richard Adams, *Watership Down* (Puffin).

3   In making recordings, on Synchrofax sheets or on tape, it is essential to preserve
         in the recorded text the pauses and intonation patterns of normal speech. Speech
         accent is not particularly important, but to slow down the speech so that every
         word has a pause after it is to destroy nearly all its value to the pupil.

Chapter 4

1   See *Exploring Language* (Edward Arnold), pp. 185–6. 'Language in use always
         involves a *context* of language, a *message* to convey, a *role* in which to convey
         it, and an *audience* to be addressed.' When all four of these are specific, and
         this is recognized by the choice of a very particular variety of language, that
         variety may be said to be using a register.
2   J. Hodgson, *Improvisation* (Methuen)
         R.M. Pemberton-Billing and J. Clegg, *Teaching Drama* (U.L.P.)
         Brian Way, *Education through Drama* (Longman)
3   P. and I. Opie, *The Lore and Language of Schoolchildren* (O.U.P.)
         P. and I. Opie, *Children's Games* (O.U.P.)
         Teachers who do not know where to start with drama could begin by asking
         their own pupils to tell them about, and demonstrate, local games and play-
         ground rituals. These books give a clear idea of what to expect.

Chapter 5

1   There is a certain mystique about remedial teaching, which is fostered by
         isolating it from the classroom where its pupils normally work. This in turn
         creates the illusion that the face-to-face encounter between remedial teacher
         and pupil is unique. Certainly there are pupils who can be helped only on a
         one-to-one basis, but the ordinary class teacher needs remedial skills as well.
         This need would point towards using peripatetic remedial specialists not as sup-
         plementary teachers but as consultants and advisory support for other teachers.
2   I.e., for children of 11, average readers once a week, less successful readers
         more frequently. In either case this refers to the child reading to the teacher,
         not to the class. See Donald Moyle, *The Teaching of Reading* (Ward Lock),
         pp. 122–4.
3   Some indications of the basis of this view can be found, among much
         speculative material, in
         H. Levin and J.P. Williams, *Basic Studies in Reading* (Basic Books, N.Y.)
         Frank Smith, *Understanding Reading* (Holt, Rinehart, and Winston)
         K.S. Goodman, *The Psycholinguistic Nature of the Reading Process* (Wayne
         State University Press).

Chapter 8

1   B. Cane and J. Smithers underline the view of most reading experts in
         suggesting that to rely on phonics *alone* or on look-and-say *alone* produces
         under-achievement in the pupil. Most other language learning calls for a
         diversity of method and approach.
2   The essential literature on this topic may be found in J. Reid (ed.), *Reading:
         Problems and Practices* (Ward Lock). One of the most useful collections of
         technical papers about reading, this anthology contains particularly valuable
         papers by the editor herself and by G.R. Roberts.

Chapter 9

1   A simple account of the *outlook* involved here can be found in C. Hannam
et al, Young Teachers and Reluctant Learners (Penguin), Chapter 6. The
special books for the Open University course 'Language and Learning',
especially Block 3, are the clearest available technical account of Bernstein's
sociolinguistic studies.

First published in Great Britain by
HarperCollins *Children's Books* in 2019
HarperCollins *Children's Books* is a division of HarperCollins*Publishers* Ltd,
HarperCollins Publishers
1 London Bridge Street
London SE1 9GF

The HarperCollins website address is
www.harpercollins.co.uk

2

Text copyright © Ben Fogle 2019
Illustrations copyright © Nikolas Ilic 2019
Cover design copyright © HarperCollins*Publishers* Ltd 2019
All rights reserved.

ISBN 978–0–00–830642–7

MR DOG

AND A HEDGE CALLED HOG

MR DOG

AND A HEDGE CALLED HOG

BEN FOGLE

with Steve Cole

Illustrated by Nikolas Ilic

HarperCollins *Children's Books*

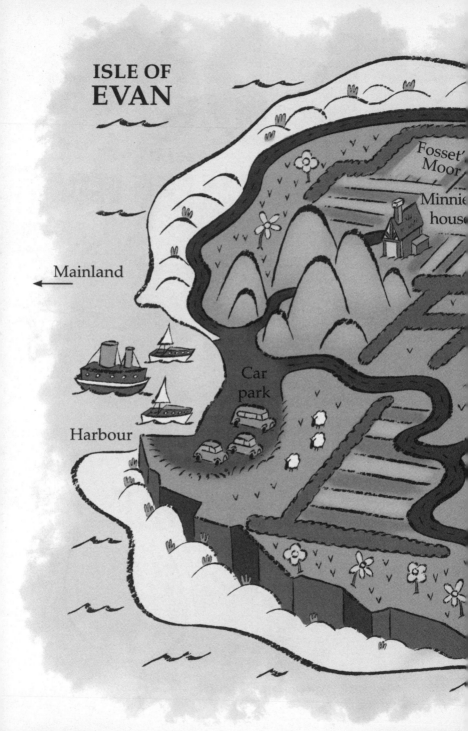

ISLE OF
EVAN

Fosset'
Moor

Minnie
house

Mainland

Car
park

Harbour

About the Author

BEN FOGLE is a broadcaster and seasoned adventurer. A modern-day nomad and journeyman, he has travelled to more than a hundred countries and accomplished amazing feats; from swimming with crocodiles to rowing three thousand miles across the Atlantic Ocean; from crossing Antarctica on foot to surviving a year as a castaway on a remote Hebridean island. Most recently, Ben climbed Mount Everest. Oh, and he LOVES dogs.

Books by Ben Fogle

MR DOG AND THE RABBIT HABIT

MR DOG AND THE SEAL DEAL

MR DOG AND A HEDGE CALLED HOG

To Otto and Ivy

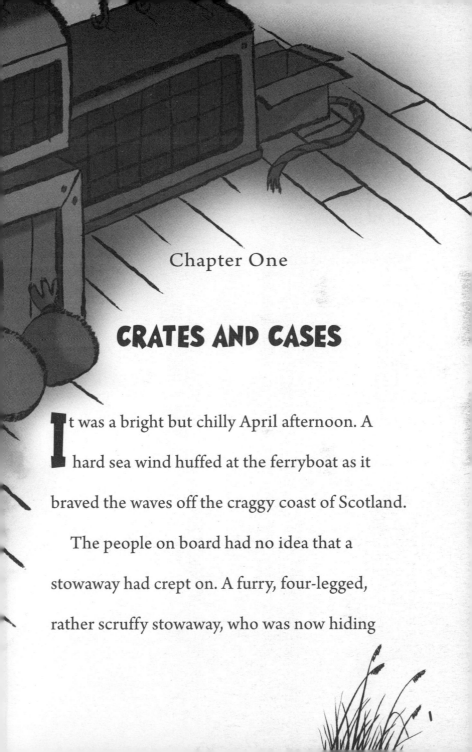

Chapter One

CRATES AND CASES

It was a bright but chilly April afternoon. A hard sea wind huffed at the ferryboat as it braved the waves off the craggy coast of Scotland.

The people on board had no idea that a stowaway had crept on. A furry, four-legged, rather scruffy stowaway, who was now hiding below deck in the cargo hold! Aside from his white beard and front paws, his fur was dark and shaggy. A ragged red-and-white hanky was tied about his neck. His ears were floppy, his nose was large and his brown eyes sparkled even in the gloom.

He wasn't just a dog. He was *Mr* Dog.

Mr Dog was a big fan of adventures, so he'd been roaming all over, from the south of England way up to the highlands of Scotland. It was there that he'd spied a group of people in a pretty little town catching the ferryboat to some islands off the coast, so he had crept into the cargo hold to go with them – and now, here he was!

To his surprise, he had found the hold mostly full of animal crates and carriers – at least forty of them. From the smell, he could tell that they had been used very recently. Some of them still had a few crushed dog biscuits inside (although with a hungry Mr Dog around, not for long). The funny thing, though, was that the crates didn't smell of dogs or cats or even of rabbits or rats, but of another animal – one that Mr Dog couldn't quite recognise. Someone had left a little fresh water in some of the bowls, so Mr Dog was glad of that.

Finally, the ferryboat slowed as it neared its destination, and Mr Dog felt the usual thrill of excitement at being about to explore somewhere

new. 'Now, how to get off without being seen?' he
mused.

Just then, the door to the hold was thrown
open. Mr Dog ducked inside a pet carrier with
solid plastic sides as a lady with frizzy blonde
hair, wearing a bright red coat, bustled inside.

'I can see Jed's pick-up truck waiting,' the lady called to one of the crew. 'He'll help me unload the empty crates.'

'Right you are, Lizzie,' a woman called back.

How kind of this Jed to help Lizzie – and to help me too! thought Mr Dog. *I may as well stay in here and be carried off in style . . .*

Sure enough, once the boat had moored up, Jed came aboard and helped frizzy-haired Lizzie shift the crates and cages out of the hold. It took several trips. Mr Dog held his breath as his own carrier was lifted up.

'This one weighs a ton!' Jed declared.

How dare you! thought Mr Dog with a secret chuckle.

As soon as his carrier was put down, Mr Dog cautiously nosed open the door and peered out. He was in the back of Jed's pick-up truck, which was as red as Lizzie's coat and parked on a pier beside a small rocky harbour. Suddenly, he heard angry voices from beside a dark green van parked close by. Lizzie was arguing with another woman, whose sharp features reminded Mr Dog of a hunting bird, and he raised his ears to listen in.

'If I'd known you were only going over to the mainland to bring back more spotlights, Mrs Maitland, I'd have thrown them overboard!' said Lizzie hotly. 'What you've been doing to those hedgies is plain cruel!'

Mr Dog was puzzled. 'Cruelty to hedgies?' he murmured. 'Whatever does she mean?'

Mrs Maitland remained calm and haughty. 'They don't belong on the Isle of Evan, Lizzie. We'll get rid of them a lot faster by hunting them down than by taking them over to the mainland in crates . . .'

'Rubbish!' Lizzie insisted. 'Your hunts are dangerous and unnecessary and they're going to stop – mark my words.'

'Are they indeed!' Mrs Maitland sneered.

'Is a hedgie like a hedge?' Mr Dog wondered aloud (although to humans, of course, it came out as *Grrr, wuff-wuff RUFF!*). He jumped down from Jed's pick-up truck and trotted past the other side of Mrs Maitland's green van, shaking his head. 'I should think it *is* unnecessary to hunt down a hedge – it just stands there and lets you find it!'

'They're not talking about hedges.' A large, sturdy tan basset hound in a thick leather collar leaned through the van window. 'They're talking about *hedgehogs.*'

'Hedgehogs!' Mr Dog grinned. 'Of course, *that* was the smell in those cages. Wait a moment. *Why* are hedgehogs being taken to the mainland? Why don't they belong on this island?'

'Who cares?' said the basset hound. 'If

Mrs Maitland says they don't, then they don't.

She's my mistress, after all.'

'So Mrs Maitland is hunting these *hedgies*?'

'No, dogs like me are hunting them.' The basset hound looked confused. 'Aren't you hunting them too?'

'Goodness, no! The only things I'm hunting are happy memories.' He raised a paw. 'I'm Mr Dog, by the way.'

'My name's Dandy.' The basset hound looked suspiciously at Mr Dog. 'I've never seen you before on the island. Did you come over from the mainland with Lizzie? Or "Lizzie Toddy, busybody", as my mistress calls her.'

Mr Dog was not impressed by name-calling. 'I did come over from the mainland,' he said, 'but not with Lizzie. I just cadged a lift in the boat.'

'Well, perhaps you'd like to join us on the hunt tonight?' said Dandy. 'It's a good chase with all the other sniffer dogs, plus it's even more fun in the dark.'

'So *that's* why you need the spotlights! Hedgehogs only come out at night.' Mr Dog sighed. He always felt sorry for an underdog – or an under*hog* in this case. 'Well, thanks for the invite to the hunt, but no thanks. I hope it all goes wonderfully well . . .' As he turned, he added quietly, 'for the hedgehogs!'

'I heard that!' Dandy's hackles rose. 'Well, just make sure you stay out of the way of my hunting pals and me . . . and don't make friends with any hedgies if you know what's good for you.'

'Perhaps I should change my name to Mr *Doog*?' Mr Dog grinned. 'Then I'd know what's *good* for me backwards!'

By now, Mrs Maitland had loaded her spotlights into her van and was clambering into the driver's seat beside Dandy. 'Stop grumbling, boy!' she snapped at his low growls. 'I'm the one who should grumble, having to deal with Lizzie Toddy, busybody ...'

Dandy barked an '*I told you so*' at Mr Dog. Then the van's engine started and Mr Dog scampered away. Mrs Maitland and Dandy drove off, then Lizzie and Jed drove away in the opposite direction.

Mr Dog trotted up the nearest grassy hillside to take a good look around at his surroundings and plan his next steps. But, really, he already knew what he was going to do.

'It sounds like the Isle of Evan's hedgies could use a good friend,' he declared. 'Luckily, good friends don't come any shaggier or waggier than Mr Dog!'

Chapter Two

A HEDGE CALLED HOG

As the sun sank lower in the sky, Mr Dog made his way through sloping meadows that were carpeted with long grass and rich with flowers.

Wind-blown trees pointed inland, to where the
fields were spread out like patchwork with thick
hedges at their edges.

'But are there any hedg*ies* in the hedges?' Mr Dog wondered aloud as he trotted onward. He wanted to warn as many of the little animals as he could about the hunt. It was a large island, though, and he didn't even know where the hunt would be taking place.

Still, I have to try, he thought.

Once Mr Dog reached the first hedge, he pushed his nose underneath. He sniffed all the way along to the next field but couldn't find any hedgehogs.

He caught a sniff of the little snufflers in the spiky hedgerow in the next field, but again he couldn't work out their location. Sleeping by day, they were well hidden and safe from sight – but not from the sniffer dogs trained to hunt them down in the darkness.

As Mr Dog was wondering what to do, he spotted a hare hopping through the waving grass. 'I say!' he called. 'Could I ask you for directions?'

'To where?' wondered the hare.

'To the nearest hedgehogs!' Mr Dog said with a grin.

The hare looked wary. 'Ah. You must be one of those hunting hounds.'

'Must I?' Mr Dog frowned. 'Why? Have you seen some hunting hounds out lately?'

'I have, yes. Out on Fosset's Moor,' the hare went on. 'I was chased by a ridgeback and a bloodhound there this morning. They told me they'd catch me if I was back again tonight. Well, not likely!'

'That's interesting.' Mr Dog wagged his tail thoughtfully. 'It sounds as if the hunt will be on Fosset's Moor.' He barked across to the hare. 'If you tell me where Fosset's Moor is, I'll tell those hounds to leave you alone!'

'Oh. Thanks, friend.' The hare thumped his back leg. 'Keep travelling east in a straight line.

Once you've climbed the hill, you'll be looking down over Fosset's Moor.'

'I'm *moor* than grateful to you!'

With a woof of farewell, Mr Dog scampered away. He ran through fields of heather, vaulted over fences, jumped over a ditch, doubled back to drink some water from the ditch, then on he ran again.

Half an hour later, as it was starting to get dark, he reached the steep hillside that the hare had described. Trotting to the top, he found a large stretch of grassland sloping away from him, lined with long, tangled rows of bushes.

'Time to investigate,' he panted, and sniffed

his way along the old, gnarled hedgerow. Many scents caught in his nostrils – honeysuckle, harvest mice, hawthorn . . . and HEDGEHOG! *Yes*, thought Mr Dog with growing excitement. It was the same smell he'd noticed in Lizzie Toddy's crates. And with night falling, the hedgies would be waking up.

Mr Dog searched about more carefully. He found a pile of damp leaves and twigs, but the long grass tickled his nose and made him sneeze.

'EEK!' the leaves seemed to squeal and Mr
Dog jumped back in surprise.

'Hello?' He got down on his belly and crawled
a little closer. 'Anyone there?'

'No,' came a quivering voice.

'Oh.' Mr Dog frowned and cocked his head.
'Are you sure no one's there?'

'ACHOO!'

'Definitely not!' said the shaky voice. 'No hedgehogs here. Only a hedge.'

Mr Dog couldn't help but smile. 'So, I'm talking to a hedge?'

'Yes, you are, and the hedge isn't talking back to you,' the voice said. 'So there.'

'Is that so?' Mr Dog replied. 'Well, thank you for letting me know.'

'You're welcome.'

'I'm welcome? In that case, I'll come back!' Mr Dog eagerly pushed his head back under the bushes. 'Hello!'

'EEK!' came the squeal again.

'There's no need to be afraid,' said Mr Dog.

'Tell me, does this hedge have a name?'

'Hog,' came the little voice.

'A hedge called Hog, eh?' Mr Dog grinned. 'You know, I think it's more likely you're a hog called Hedge!'

'No! My name *is* Hog, honest . . .' In the twilight, Mr Dog saw a little black nose push out from the leaves. Two beady black eyes and a spiky fringe followed close behind. Before he knew it, Mr Dog was snout to snout with a young hedgehog!

'EEP!' Hog's eyes widened with alarm and, in a heartbeat, he rolled himself up into a spiky ball.

Mr Dog blinked. 'Goodness, I wish I could

do a trick like that. Although then I suppose I'd

have to call myself Mr *Hog* instead of Mr Dog.'

'Whoever you are, you're scary,' said

Hog, trembling.

'*Hairy*, yes. Scary, never,' said Mr Dog. 'The D-O-G in my name stands for Delightful Old Gentleman! Well, probably.'

'My mum told me about dogs!' Hog's quills quivered as he spoke. 'She told me that the two-legged giants take sniffy dogs and go hunting for hedgies.'

'I think you mean "sniffer" dogs,' said Mr Dog.

'The sniffing sniffy sniffer dogs sniff us out, and the giants sweep sticks through the long grass and poke us hedgies into the open.' Hog gave a long, snuffling sigh. 'And we're never seen again.'

'What a terrible story! Wait.' Mr Dog reversed

out from under the hedgerow and sniffed the air. 'I can smell something . . .'

'Maybe it's an escaping hedgehog!' Hog squealed and beetled away along the side of the hedgerow, heading down the hillside. 'Goodbye, scary dog! I'm off!'

'Hog, come back!' It had grown dark, but Mr Dog's senses were keen. His nose was filling with wet, animal smells. At the same time, he saw bright lights bobbing up the hill towards him, the same way he'd come. There were noises too: a thumping, crashing sound and excited yelps. Hounds – and lots of them.

'Good boy, Dandy!' Mrs Maitland's voice

carried through the darkness. 'Have you found one? Found a hedgehog for us . . . ?'

'Oh, dear!' Mr Dog ran down the hill after the little hedgehog as the crashing got closer. 'The hunt is coming, Hog – and I'm afraid they're hunting you!'

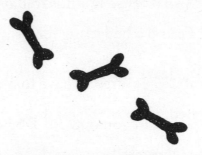

Chapter Three

A FIGHT IN THE NIGHT!

Mr Dog soon caught up with Hog, who was beetling towards the nearest hedgerow. 'You led the hunt to me!' he squealed, prickles rippling over his body as he ran. 'You're a big, mean sniffy dog!'

'I did not lead anyone to you,' Mr Dog

insisted. 'And if those hounds find us, you'll have the proof. Now, keep running!'

'I can't!' Hog puffed. 'I have to hide!'

'They will sniff you out,' Mr Dog told him. 'We have to outrun them.'

It sounded as if the scrum of people and hounds was crashing ever closer to the top of the hill. The lights blazed into view like an approaching fire, turning the dark fields floodlit, and the yips and barks of the dogs rose in pitch.

'Dandy, no!' Mrs Maitland shouted crossly. 'Come back here!'

Mr Dog gasped as a familiar figure jumped into sight over the hill. Dandy the basset hound had escaped his owner to pursue the hedgehog alone, his lead trailing behind him.

'Faster! Faster! Must run faster!' Hog repeated the words over and over, his little paws tearing across the turf.

Mr Dog knew that the hedgehog was just too slow.

Dandy only had little legs himself, but he was closing fast. 'Curl up, Hog, quickly!'

With a desperate squeal, Hog tucked himself into a ball. Mr Dog turned and reared up on his back legs to block the basset hound, but Dandy dodged him and then – BAM! – swiped at Hog with the side of his head. In so doing, Dandy got a cheekful of prickles and yelped.

Mr Dog saw poor Hog bounce and bump away down the hillside like a football. Angrily,

he pushed his head under Dandy's low-hanging stomach and flipped the hound over, barking as scarily as he could. Caught off-guard, his cheek still stinging, Dandy backed away. The baying hounds were very close now, straining forward with their handlers. Mrs Maitland led the charge, grabbing Dandy's lead before he could escape again.

'A dog helping a hedgehog instead of his own kind?' Dandy snarled. 'You'll regret this, scruff-bag. My pals and I will get you, just you wait!'

'Sorry, no time to wait!' Mr Dog bounded away after Hog. 'I've a talking hedge to look out for!'

Hog had tumbled down to the bottom of

the hill and was lying on his back with his eyes closed, panting for breath. He looked to be in a total daze.

Mr Dog cast a nervous look back at the pack of dogs hurrying down the hill towards them. Each bark was like a blade slicing through the night. 'There's no time to lose,' he murmured. Carefully, Mr Dog closed his jaws round Hog, lifted him up and ran away. He ducked through a hedgerow and sped across a fallow field, putting as much distance as he could between himself and the hunting party. *On the lead, those dogs can only move as fast as their handlers,* he thought. *They shouldn't be too hard to outrun!*

But Mr Dog could hear the warning in the
howls the pack threw after him: '*We won't always
be on the lead. Just you wait, scruff-bag – we're
going to get you and that hog . . . and there'll be no
humans to stop us!*'

Mr Dog carried Hog delicately between his

teeth for what had to be more than a mile

before finally he stopped on high ground further

round the coast. His jaws were aching and his

tongue was sore from prickles. Trying not to

pant, he listened hard but could hear only the

roar of the sea below, crashing on rocks

somewhere in the darkness beneath.

The stars were bright and the moon was up now, and full. Mr Dog padded over to a hunched-over tree and gently placed Hog beneath it on a bed of leaves. As far as he could tell, the little hedgie was uninjured. To keep Hog safe, he covered him over with more leaves and then lay down beside him, exhausted.

Soon Mr Dog fell into an uneasy sleep, ears twitching for any sound of the hounds. He was fond himself of hunting about after interesting smells, and knew that some hounds – particularly in more remote places – were bred to do nothing else. However, he knew that a few liked to hunt

so much that they got overexcited, determined to catch their prey whatever it took. That made them dangerous to anyone who got in their way.

He jumped at the sound of movement beside him, but it was only Hog wriggling into sight through the leaves.

'Oh, what horrible dreams I've had,' squealed the hedgehog. He sniffed and stared about. 'Where are my friends? Where am I?'

'I wish I knew,' said Mr Dog. 'I'm a stranger here myself.'

'Aaaagh!' Hog squealed like a little siren going off. 'It's you! I remember. You tried to eat me!'

'I only picked you up so I could carry you to

safety!' Mr Dog let his tongue dangle from his mouth. 'I got prickled by a prickle too.'

But the little hedgie was in another panic. 'I won't let you bite me!' His tiny legs propelled him out of the leaves and he scurried up the grassy slope towards a rocky ledge. 'I'm off!'

'Hog, wait,' Mr Dog yelped. 'It's not safe!'

The panicking hedgehog was running straight for the edge of a cliff!

Chapter Four

HELPING HOG

Mr Dog raced after him and barked, 'STOP!'
Such was the power in that ear-shaking

woof that the hedgehog jumped, skidded and

spun round. He found himself on one paw,

teetering on the edge of a long drop down to the

rocky shoreline far below.

'Eep!' Hog
shut his eyes.
'Come here,
small one.' Mr Dog's
teeth once again closed
gently round Hog's middle,
lifted him from the dangerous
ledge and carried him down
to safety. The moment Mr Dog
placed him back on the ground,

Hog tucked himself back into a trembling ball.

'We're close to the cliffs, you silly spiky thing,' Mr Dog scolded. 'You really must trust me. I'm a friend to all animals.'

'All right.' Hog poked out his nose and opened one eye. 'I'm sorry if I was rude. But you sniffy dogs are very scary to a little hedge like me. Not just your teeth. Those dirty great paws of yours could squash me flat.'

'Dirty paws? How dare you! I'm extremely clean.' Mr Dog wiped his front paws in the dew and kicked up some grass with the back ones. 'See? I promise not to squash you, Hog. I just want to get you to safety. Now where do you live – under that hedgerow?'

'Nope. I don't really have a home.' Small tears welled up in Hog's beady black eyes. 'I usually just wander about, sometimes with my friends. But that was until something awful happened . . .'

Mr Dog lay down beside him. 'Tell me about it.'

'I was out with some friends, looking for food,' Hog went on, unfolding himself as he talked. 'Sprackle said that he knew a field full of caterpillars, and Tucker thought we might even find some wader eggs.'

'From wader birds?' Mr Dog was surprised. 'You eat eggs?'

42

'Well, not me personally,' Hog admitted. 'But Sprackle and Tucker think they're the most delicious food ever. We thought that hunting for some would be a good adventure.' He snuffled quietly. 'But fog blew in from the sea and I lost my way. I couldn't find Sprackle and Tucker. Then I heard them cry out for help . . .' Hog quivered so much he almost curled up again. 'I looked for them, but couldn't see them anywhere. When the sun came up, I hid under that hedgerow and slept.'

Mr Dog nodded sympathetically. 'What about your family? Where are they?'

'I've no idea,' said Hog. 'A hoglet leaves his

family behind when he's five or six weeks, and

I'm nearly four seasons old now.'

'Well, Hog, they do say that travel broadens

the mind, and I'm sure it sharpens the prickles

too.' Mr Dog wagged his shaggy broom of a tail.

'I'm here to help you. Perhaps we can find—'

Hog sprang up in the air. 'A BEETLE.'

Mr Dog was confused. 'Well, I suppose we could find a beetle, but I actually meant—'

'No, I mean, I just heard a beetle.' Hog was already snuffling away through the grass, licking his lips. 'Mmmm, come to me, beetle . . . OM, NOM, NOM!' He munched the insect down. 'It may not be a wader egg . . . but it's delicious!'

Mr Dog smiled down at the scatty little hedgie. He wondered what on earth cute animals like this had done to get Mrs Maitland cross enough to send out hunting parties. '*They don't belong on the Isle of Evan,*' she'd said – but WHY didn't they?

'As I was saying,' Mr Dog went on, 'perhaps we could find a lady called Lizzie Toddy who lives on this island. She came over on the same boat as me and she seemed to like hedgehogs.'

'What's a boat?' Hog asked.

'It's a thing humans use to travel over water,' Mr Dog explained. 'Lizzie had all sorts of crates and cases for carrying hedgehogs, and wanted to stop the hunt. Perhaps if we find her, she will help you.'

Hog looked up at Mr Dog, his black eyes wide and bright. 'Do you really think she would?'

'I think it's worth a try.' Mr Dog sighed. 'Unfortunately, I have no idea where she is or

46

how we can find her.' He brightened, licking his chops. 'Still, the island can't be that big, can it? And she was in a big red pick-up, so she must live near a road . . .'

'Roads are a bit scary,' said Hog. 'They have big metal things on them that roar and try to squish you.'

'We'll take extra care,' Mr Dog assured him. Then he held up a paw for quiet. Distantly, blown on the wind, he could hear the bark and yap of excited hounds. 'Uh-oh. Sounds like the pack is back.'

'EEEEP!' Hog had already rolled himself up into a ball.

Mr Dog smiled down at the little hedgehog. 'We'd better get moving.'

Hog pushed out his nose. 'But where to?' he twittered.

'Perhaps down to the beach.' Mr Dog walked carefully back to the ledge of the cliff and surveyed the steep descent. 'A dog can manage a tough climb, but the hounds' human handlers won't want to chance it. They'll hopefully give up and leave us be—'

'Leave us BEETLE?' said Hog excitedly.

Mr Dog frowned. 'No. Just leave us be.'

'Oh.' Hog stuck out his tongue. 'Bees don't taste very nice. I much prefer beetles.'

'Escape first,' said Mr Dog, 'beetles later.' He paused. 'Do you think you could try not to curl up while I carry you? My tongue could use a rest from prickles.'

Hog shifted uncomfortably but nodded. Mr Dog delicately picked him up in his jaws and set off, taking a careful path down the steep, muddy hillside. The dark sea frothed and hissed as it slapped against the strip of stony beach that huddled between this cliff face and the next. Surely the hunters couldn't possibly follow their hedgehog trail down here!

Mr Dog was just congratulating himself on his cleverness when a tuft of turf gave way beneath him.

He scrabbled at the wet mud and rock but

couldn't get a paw-hold, and started sliding down

the steep slope towards the sea!

'What's happening?' squeaked Hog.

'Hold on!' Mr Dog groaned through a

mouthful of prickles, paws still scrabbling at

stone and grass as he picked up speed. 'Looks

like we're taking the quick way down!'

Chapter Five

EGG-STRA SPECIAL

Mr Dog gave a howl of fear as he slid faster down towards the stony beach. Suddenly, he hit a grassy outcrop that sent him tumbling head-over-paws. To his horror, Hog had slipped from his mouth! The little hedgehog was bouncing off a boulder and flying up into the air. Mr Dog spread out his legs beneath the airborne hedgehog and flattened himself down on the ground to catch him. He gave a sigh of relief as the hedgie landed on his back!

'EEEEP!' Hog's little teeth chomped into Mr Dog's necktie and he clung on for dear life.

A jagged rock sticking out from the cliff face loomed in front of Mr Dog. Desperately, he pushed off from the rock with his paws to avoid hitting it full-on . . .

For a few moments, all he could feel was cold air ruffling through his fur, nothingness beneath his paws, and then . . .

Mr Dog and Hog plunged into freezing water.

Everything was black, and all noise was muffled.

Doggy-paddling furiously, he broke the surface

of the water. The sea roared in his ears and the air

was filled with salty spray.

'Hog?' barked Mr Dog. 'Where are you?'

'Right here!' came the little squeak of a voice

in his ear. Hog was still clinging on with paws and

jaws to Mr Dog, shaking with fright. 'What is this

giant, angry, salty puddle?'

'It's the sea,' Mr Dog spluttered, striking out

for shore. 'It's all around the island.'

'The sea? I see. Mr Dog, are you my boat?'

'That's right, Hog! Just hold on tight and we'll

be back on dry land in two shakes of a soggy tail!'

Swimming with all his might, Mr Dog reached

the pebbly shore and dragged himself onto it.

His body felt bruised and sore, and his tummy

was red with scratches from the long slide down.

Hog clambered over Mr Dog's head on to the wet

beach. Then he waddled round and squeezed up

against him, shivering with the cold. Mr Dog put

a protective paw over him, his pads shielding him

from the prickles.

They lay like that for a few minutes, then

Mr Dog got up and led them to shelter at the

base of the cliffs. High above, he could hear the

yips and yaps of the hounds, and saw the blazing

beams of the humans' hand-held searchlights.

'I don't suggest you follow us down here!' Mr Dog muttered.

After a few minutes, the searchlights faded and the barking died away. The hunters had moved away from the ledge.

'What do we do now?' asked Hog through tiny chattering teeth.

Mr Dog considered. It was an impossible climb back up. 'I think we had better try to walk round the shoreline for a while. It'll keep us out of the way of those hounds at least!'

Luckily, the tide was going out, so by splashing through the rockpools at the edge of the little cove, carrying Hog between his teeth, Mr Dog was able to reach the neighbouring beach. Mr Dog walked across the lonely stretch of sand, the sea hurling spray as it surged in and then hissed back out. He stopped for a brief rest, and looked at the craggy solitude around him. The sky was lightening, and seabirds wheeled and called from the cliffs as they woke and began their days.

Hog yawned. 'I should be asleep,' he said.

'That's why we have to keep moving now,' Mr Dog explained. 'The hounds won't be looking for you in daylight. It gives us more time to find Lizzie.'

But Hog wasn't listening. He had fallen asleep

on the sand, snuffling and snoring. With a smile,
Mr Dog gently picked up the little hedgie with
his teeth and, with some difficulty, tucked him
inside his red-and-white neckerchief. Then he set
off again.

The day warmed up as Mr Dog made his way
round the coast, his tiny rider puffing in his ear
with each snoozing breath. Eventually, the cliffs
gave way to lower-lying dunes lined with sea kelp.
A beautiful scent teased Mr Dog's nose, and as
he climbed to the top of the dunes he found a
spectacular carpet of wild flowers of all different
colours: vivid reds, cheery yellows and bold
purples. Sand flies spun in a haze above the

flowers, and the sweet-smelling grass seemed

alive with insects. That perhaps explained the

sheer number of wader birds gliding and striding

about – Mr Dog spotted dunlins and plovers and

coots and many more he didn't recognise. The air
was filled with trills and tweets and piping calls
of strange and unusual breeds.

Then he spotted some wooden shelters set
up further inland with slits in the walls. *Hides,*
thought Mr Dog. *Human bird-watchers must
use the hides to watch the birds here without
disturbing them. I suppose there must be* rare
birds around here.

Thirsty and hungry from all his exertions, Mr Dog lapped some dew from the grass beside a small mound. A bird with a bright red neck burst out from behind it with a sharp, screeching cry, and Mr Dog jumped. Then he noticed a small, untidy nest in the flowery grass. Four splotchy olive eggs sat inside it.

Hog started to wriggle in the grip of his raggedy collar. 'Ooooh! What's that whiff in my nose?' The little hedgie pulled himself free and dropped down to the fragrant turf. 'Oooooh, something smells delicious.'

Mr Dog frowned. 'The eggs, you mean?'

'EGGS!' Hog wiggled towards the eggs with

startling speed. 'At last. My friends said wader eggs were the best. Now I can taste them for myself!'

'Hog, wait!' Mr Dog stuck his nose right up to the hedgehog and nudged him aside. 'You shouldn't eat that egg. There's a little chick growing inside it!'

Hog tried to push past Mr Dog, his mouth watering. 'Pardon?'

'Well, would you like it if a bird ate a little baby hoglet?' Mr Dog demanded. 'Eat a bug or a beetle instead. They lay many more eggs at a time.'

'But hedgehogs are *always* eating bird eggs,' Hog protested. 'They're this island's top tasty treat! We've been eating them for ages.'

Mr Dog gasped. 'Hog . . . perhaps that's it!'

'That's what?' said Hog, puzzled.

'The reason you hedgies are being hunted,'

said Mr Dog gravely. 'I think I've worked it out!'

Chapter Six

DANGER IN THE FIELDS

'**Y**ou told me that you hedgehogs keep eating wader eggs,' Mr Dog reminded Hog. 'Well, I'm a well-travelled animal and I don't recognise a lot of the birds here. I think there must be many rare breeds – which means they only lay their eggs in a very few places . . .'

'Oh. Oh, dear. I see what you're saying.' Hog looked up at Mr Dog, wide-eyed and prickles pointing. 'If hedgehogs eat all those eggs, there'll be no more new chicks hatching.'

'And the rare birds get even rarer,' Mr Dog agreed. 'The humans could be trying to protect them.'

'By getting rid of hedgies?' said Hog sadly. 'But we're only following our instincts. How could we know that some of these eggs are special?'

'I know,' said Mr Dog. 'And I still don't understand what Mrs Maitland meant when she said you hedgehogs didn't belong here.'

'It makes me want to hide away forever.' Hog looked up at Mr Dog. 'Perhaps I could pretend

to be a hedge again? I know I didn't fool you, but then you are *extra* clever.'

'True.' Mr Dog grinned. 'But I don't think anyone will believe you're a hedge. Now, come on. We have to try and find Lizzie Toddy "Busybody", and hope she's not *too* busy to help you and your friends!'

Mr Dog let Hog fill up on insects and caterpillars, and even munched on a couple of crickets himself. Then he carried the little hedgehog away through the thick carpet of flowers. A stream cut through the moorland, sloping sandy banks on each side. At last Mr Dog could drink and bathe the sore spots on his tongue from all of Hog's prickles.

They travelled along the hedgerows, so Hog could warn any hedgies hiding there to watch out for dogs, and Mr Dog could demonstrate what a dog actually looked like. By the middle of the afternoon, Hog had snuffled out the hiding places of twenty-seven hedgehogs and had had a

quiet word with each, telling them to keep close to cover, avoid eggs and pass on the information to other hedgehogs.

'One last thing,' Hog said solemnly at the end of every warning. 'Don't pretend to be a talking hedge – it doesn't seem to work!'

As they walked through the fields, Mr Dog kept his ear cocked for sounds of traffic, but there were none.

'The nearest road could be miles away,' Mr Dog muttered.

'Why are roads so important?' asked Hog, looking up at him.

'They lead to farms and houses. I might pick

up Lizzie's scent on a road – or even spot her pick-up truck out and about. After all, this is only a small island.'

He spoke with as much confidence as he could, trying to reassure the little hedgehog. But really he knew they might wander the island together, lost, for days and nights. In the meantime, for all the hedgehogs they were warning, many more would be hunted by hounds and be at Mrs Maitland's mercy.

They stopped for a rest in a grassy field in which small sheep with black faces and brown tufty coats were grazing. The nearest ewes backed away at the sight of Mr Dog. One of

them, braver than the rest, stamped a hoof.

'I'm too tired to chase you,' Mr Dog assured her.

'Hey, are you thirsty?' Hog was peering across the field and sniffing the air. 'I think there's a stream around here.'

'There is.' With his keener eyesight, Mr Dog could see the stream, cutting through the bottom of the field. Then he heard something – a low chugging and popping noise. It sounded like an engine!

'Get into a ball, Hog,' Mr Dog instructed. 'An engine means a vehicle – and that means a road. We need to see where it's coming from.'

The hedgehog curled up and rolled neatly into

Mr Dog's jaws. 'I'm good to go!'

Mr Dog picked up Hog and hared away in

search of the vehicle. He sent sheep

scattering as he galloped past,

and mumbled apologies.

The noise of the engine grew

louder. At the bottom of the field stood an open

gate, and Mr Dog saw an old, muddy tractor

rumbling into view on enormous wheels.

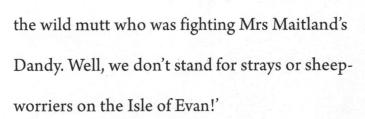

'We'll take the direction it came from,' he decided, and changed course towards the tractor. But then the tractor stopped and its driver dropped down from inside, looking very angry!

'Chase my flock, would you?' The farmer, tall, lean and red-faced, pointed at Mr Dog, who skidded to a stop. 'You must be the wild mutt who was fighting Mrs Maitland's Dandy. Well, we don't stand for strays or sheep-worriers on the Isle of Evan!'

'I'm not wild – I'm really quite reasonable,'

Mr Dog protested. 'And your sheep aren't worried, they're just a little surprised!' But of course, his words came out just as woofs and wuffs to the farmer, and all muffled by a mouthful of hedgie. To Mr Dog's horror, the farmer reached inside the tractor's cab – and pulled out a shotgun.

'Goodbye!' Mr Dog turned tail and ran as fast as he could in the opposite direction, heading for the stream. BOOM! The shotgun fired. Mr Dog's eyes widened but he kept on running.

'EEEEP! What was that?' cried Hog.

'Nothing nice!' Mr Dog told him. Heart hammering, he put on a last desperate burst of speed. BOOM! The farmer fired again.

Sand sprayed from the bank just in front of Mr Dog and showered over him. Some went in his eyes. Blinded for a moment, he leaped for cover, tumbled down the bank and hit the stream.

The splash-landing knocked Hog from out of Mr Dog's jaws! With an 'EEEEEEP!' and a PLOP, the hedgehog hit the cold blue water . . . and sank from sight!

'Hog?' Mr Dog pushed his face into the water and blinked, trying to clear his eyes. 'Oh, Hog! What have I done?' He searched about more desperately. 'That poor prickled pickle – I've lost him in the water. He'll be drowned!'

Chapter Seven

ON THE ROAD

Mr Dog grew desperate, splashing about in a circle, looking for Hog. The farmer's voice carried across the field and over the bank, 'What's all that splashing? Did I hit him . . . ?'

Not yet, you didn't, thought Mr Dog. *And I'm*

not going to give you another chance! He knew he

had to leave. 'Oh, Hog . . .'

'Quickly, Mr Dog,' came a high, twittery voice

from the hedgerow on the far side of the stream.

'We must go!'

'What?' Mr Dog shook water from his ears.

'Who said that?'

'Well, it's not the hedge,

is it?' A familiar little

face with eyes as

black as his nose

pushed out from

the greenery.

'Hog!' Mr Dog

leaped from the water and gave his little friend a fond lick on the side of the face – before yelping at the sting of prickles. 'How did you get out of the water?'

Hog blinked. 'Didn't you know hedgehogs could swim?'

'No!' exclaimed Mr Dog.

'Well, neither did I,' Hog admitted. 'But we can! So I did. I swam right between your back legs and then crawled out to the hedgerow. I called to you but you were too busy splashing about. Now, come on!'

Mr Dog turned back to the field and stood up on his legs to see over the bank. The farmer was

striding towards the stream with his gun. 'You're quite right, Hog. We must go at once.' He dug furiously at the sandy turf with his paws, trying to make a space big enough to fit through.

Hog tried to help, but was soon buried in a pile of sand! He pulled himself free and beetled through to the other side of the hedge. 'Oooh! Mr Dog, I spy a winding grey thing. I think it's a road.'

'Really?' Mr Dog squeezed and squashed through his little trench beneath the hedgerow and joined Hog on the other side. A narrow, single-track road full of bumps and potholes stretched alongside the farmer's field. 'You're right, Hog, it IS a road – and we'd better take it!'

Mr Dog grabbed Hog and tossed him in the air. Hog rolled up into a ball and Mr Dog made a perfect catch with his jaws – then took off at high speed. BOOM! Thunder burst from the farmer's shotgun one more time, but Mr Dog kept running until he was safely out of sight round the corner. Then he paused, panting for breath as he placed Hog back on the ground.

'Was that human trying to hurt you?' asked the hedgehog.

'I'm afraid so. He must've been on the hunt last night – he saw me fight off Dandy the basset, and now he thinks I'm a menace to other

animals, like his sheep.' Mr Dog sighed. 'Farmers have to guard their flocks well in isolated spots, as help is so hard to come by.'

'So is help for hedgehogs,' said Hog sadly.

The two friends continued along the road, Mr Dog wanting to put a safe distance between himself and the farmer. Hog lay draped over Mr Dog's back, snoring now and then as he snoozed. The clouds were starting to darken in the late-afternoon sky when the sound of another engine thrummed through the landscape. A car was coming!

Mr Dog quickly hid among the long grass and buttercups at the side of the road, afraid it

might be the farmer. But no, this was a red Land
Rover driven by an old woman, towing a trailer
loaded with chopped-up logs for firewood. As
the Land Rover rattled past, Mr Dog waited,
poised to spring.

'Hold on tight,' he told Hog. Then he ran out
and, with a majestic leap, landed in the trailer on
the logs.

'**WHEEE!**' cried Hog through a mouthful of neckerchief as he clung to Mr Dog's back. 'That was an amazing jump.'

'I believe I was a racehorse in a former life,' said Mr Dog with a chuckle. 'Now we can travel further, faster – and in style!'

The road wound along through fields and moors, and Mr Dog watched them go by, quietly regaining his strength. But as the trailer turned left at a junction and trundled past a stretch of woodland, he caught a sudden sniff of danger.

Hog stiffened beside him, nose twitching too. 'I recognise that smell . . .'

Ahead of them, Dandy the basset was pushing out from the forest edge. Just behind him came three more dogs – a harrier, a bloodhound and a ridgeback.

'It's the hounds from last night!' Mr Dog flattened himself down over the logs in the trailer. 'They said I'd regret picking your side . . .'

Hog was shaking. 'You mean they're roaming free, and looking for us?'

Dandy sniffed the air – then turned sharply towards the trailer. His floppy ears practically stood on end as he saw Mr Dog.

'They're not looking for us, Hog,' said Mr Dog grimly. 'I'm afraid they've *found* us!'

'There he is!' Dandy howled. 'I can smell that hedgehog too. After them!'

The hounds came charging after the trailer, barking and yapping. Mr Dog saw the fury in Dandy's face. *I normally get on terribly well with bassets,* he reflected. *It just goes to show: there are no mean dog breeds – only mean dogs.*

'We're going too fast for them,' Hog realised as the car accelerated away. The angry hounds grew smaller and smaller, until they were lost from view round the next corner. 'They can't catch up! Yay!'

'What a relief,' Mr Dog agreed – just as the old lady's car began to slow down again. 'Oh, no!' Up ahead he could see that some cattle were being led from one field to another. They were completely blocking the road. 'We'll be stuck here for ages.'

'That means that Dandy and the others will catch up with us.' Hog had already curled into a ball. 'Oh, no. Oh, EEEP! They're going to get us!'

Chapter Eight

INTO THE WOODS

As the old lady's car slowed down further, Mr Dog made a quick decision. 'I've enjoyed the ride, but I think this is our stop. Come on, Hog!' Mr Dog snatched up Hog and made an enormous leap from the still-moving trailer, clear over the top of a big clump of nettles. Hitting the ground running, he disappeared into the woods.

'But they're sniffy dogs, Mr Dog!' Hog squeaked. 'Won't they just follow your trail?'

'My scent will be stronger in the trailer,' Mr Dog panted. 'I jumped the bush so I wouldn't leave an obvious track. Hopefully by the time they realise we're not hiding in the old lady's log pile, we'll have a good head start!'

The four hounds came yapping and barking round the corner. The trailer had stopped moving by now, and Dandy put on a burst of speed on his sturdy little legs, eager to catch up. But the cattle saw the dogs running at them and started to mill about in alarm, mooing. The farmer frowned and shouted a warning at the dogs. The harrier and the bloodhound held back, but Dandy and the ridgeback jumped on to the trailer, sniffing about furiously. The old woman got out of her car and started waving her arms at them, shooing them out.

'So far, so good,' said Mr Dog as Hog scrambled on to his back. 'But we must keep moving.'

'Where are we going?' Hog wondered, biting hard on to Mr Dog's red spotted neckerchief to hold on.

'For now, anywhere that Dandy and his friends are not,' said Mr Dog. 'It's the only way to keep you safe.'

The pair set off again. Mr Dog's legs ached, but he didn't dare stop. He knew the hounds would be able to pick up even a faint trail, given enough time. To his relief, he chanced upon a stream running through the wood and drank thirstily. 'We must travel on through the water,' he said. 'That way, we'll leave no trail or scent at all.'

'Clever!' Hog jumped into the stream and started paddling away. 'You need a rest from carrying me. I'll swim alongside you.'

Mr Dog gave him a grin and splashed into the water after him. 'Nothing like an afternoon swim when you're all hot and dusty, eh?'

They set off through the stream, but Mr Dog's

good mood didn't last long. He could already hear the yap of Dandy and the hounds in the distance.

The day was turning to dusk, and Hog began to tire. Mr Dog lifted him up, dripping, from the water and jumped out on to the bank, being careful to leave no tracks.

'Where are we going to go, Mr Dog?' asked Hog. 'Where can a little hedgie like me find safety?'

'We'll find somewhere,' Mr Dog told him. 'What we need is someone local . . . someone who knows the area . . .'

'You called, pets?' came a high, wavery voice from behind them. 'If it's safety for hedgies you're after, I may be able to help!'

The voice seemed to belong to the stump of a tree. Mr Dog gently dropped Hog as another hedgehog popped up. It was a very plump and elderly hedgehog, her prickles grey but her eyes bright with wisdom.

'How do you do,' said Mr Dog politely. 'I'm Mr

Dog and this is Hog. And what is your name, may

I ask?'

'I'm Maura,' said the old hedgie. 'I am forty

seasons old.' She smiled proudly. 'In hedgehog

years, that's about one hundred and four!'

Mr Dog's jaw dropped. 'To have lived for so long, you must know all the best places for a hedgie to hide!'

'Not only that, pet. I happen to be very well bred.' Maura raised her little twitchy nose up in the air. 'I am descended from the very first hedgehogs on the Isle of Evan.'

'The very first?' Hog marvelled. 'How do you know?'

'Because the very first hedgehogs on this island were brought across from the mainland over a thousand seasons ago,' Maura explained. 'The lady who owns these lands wanted hedgies

to eat the slugs and snails in her garden. Well,

they did, of course, as hedgies do. And in time,

they had little hoglets, and those hoglets grew up

and *they* had hoglets . . .'

Mr Dog nodded. 'So the hedgehog population grew and grew.'

Hog was fidgeting. 'Um, please, Mr Dog, shouldn't we be finding that place to hide?'

'Soon, Hog. I think we're learning the reason why hedgehogs have to hide at all.' Mr Dog turned back to Maura and grinned. 'The D-O-G in my surname is short for "DO-Go on" . . . !'

'Thank you, pet. I shall.' Maura seemed pleased. 'With quiet roads, no predators and a huge amount of delicious wader eggs nearby, it was a hedgie paradise. My ancestors were the first to be brought here, yes, but soon there were thousands of hedgies on the Isle of Evan.'

'And that must have affected the other wildlife,' Mr Dog realised.

'Like the wader birds!' Hog wheezed in alarm. 'It's like you said, Mr Dog. The birds were always able to hatch their eggs here safely until us hedgies came along and started to eat them . . .'

Mr Dog nodded sadly. 'I hate to say it, but it sounds as if Mrs Maitland was right – hedgehogs *don't* belong on the Isle of Evan.'

Maura bristled. 'It's not my family's fault we were kidnapped and set to work here, is it?'

'It's not any hedgehog's fault,' Hog agreed.

'No, it isn't,' said Mr Dog. 'Which is why

Lizzie Toddy "Busybody" is trying to deal with the situation kindly, even while Mrs Maitland and her friends are hunting you down.'

'Lizzie Toddy, you say?' Maura nodded. 'Why, these woods back on to her garden, pet. Her farm is the safe place I was going to tell you about!'

'Marvellous,' woofed Mr Dog. 'Which way do we go? I'm all ears!' And he shook his shaggy ears about to prove it. As he did so, he heard distant snorting and yapping from somewhere in the woods.

'You'd better tell us fast, Maura,' said Hog. 'Some hounds are coming. They must've picked up our scent.'

'You'll be in danger too, Maura,' Mr Dog realised.

'In my younger days, I could climb this tree,' Maura said wistfully. 'Hedgies are quite the climbers, you know! But as it is, I'll just curl up.' She demonstrated, revealing her hundreds of extra-spiky prickles. 'No dog's silly enough to bother me! Tatty-bye, pets!'

'Wait! Which way do we go?' Mr Dog pawed the ground in front of her. 'You haven't told us yet!'

'No time!' Hog cried, beetling away towards the cover of a nearby bush. 'Run for it, Mr Dog!' But as he vanished under the leaves, there came a clang of metal and a frightened 'EEEP!'

Mr Dog dashed over and bit at the bush's branches. They came away easily to reveal an old rusted cage of wire mesh beneath. 'A vermin trap!' he breathed. Some of the bars were bent, leaving a gap – not quite enough to let a hedgie get out, but enough for determined paws to get in.

'I can't leave you here, Hog,' said Mr Dog.

'Dandy and his friends might get you.'

Hog was shivering with fear. 'But if you stay,

they'll get us both for sure!'

Chapter Nine

ATTACK FROM ABOVE!

Mr Dog had come across traps like this before.

The cage door had closed as Hog blundered inside and brushed against the catch. Now it was jammed tight and, though he bit at the

rusty bars and pulled with all his strength, he couldn't budge it.

The sound of the hounds crashing through the undergrowth was getting louder.

'I'll try to lead them away,' Mr Dog told Hog, nudging the branches back over the cage. 'Hopefully they'll chase after me and lose your scent. I'll circle round and get back to you just as soon as I can.'

Hog was rocking from side to side. 'But what if they catch you?'

'I'm quick on my paws,' Mr Dog assured him. But then he heard the sound of something bigger and larger thumping through the woods.

'What's this?' A woman with blonde frizzy hair, red gardening gloves and a red coat came running into sight. 'I thought I heard woofing and the scream of a frightened hedgie . . .' She scowled at Mr Dog. 'Get away from that cage! Go on, shoo!'

Me? thought Mr Dog indignantly.

Lizzie pulled the cage from under the bush. 'My old trap caught the hedgie before you could hurt him, thank goodness.' She looked up at the sound of Dandy and his pack-mates crashing through the bracken, then back at Mr Dog. 'You can't have this hedgie. Go on, get back to your friends.'

'They're no friends of mine, madam!' Mr Dog protested, but of course to her it only sounded like woofing, and seemed to make her crosser. She lifted the cage to head height out of any animal's reach, wedged it in the fork of two sturdy branches in Maura's tree and opened the door, ready to scoop Hog out from inside.

'Get off me!' squealed Hog, wriggling away from her fingers. 'Help!'

'She won't hurt you, Hog,' barked Mr Dog. 'This is Lizzie, she wants to help . . .'

Lizzie looked again at Mr Dog. 'Wait a moment. Hey, didn't I see you at the harbour yesterday? Are you the stray dog that Moaning Minnie Maitland's been on about?'

Mr Dog quickly sat down and offered a paw as a show of friendship.

She looked at him thoughtfully. 'You don't seem very wild and dangerous to me . . .'

'But those hounds are!' Hog was looking through the bars of his cage and trembling. 'Run,

106

Mr Dog! The sniffy dogs are coming!'

The next moment, Dandy came thundering through the undergrowth, barking ferociously. Mr Dog reared up in alarm, and the ridgeback came flying at him and knocked him over backwards. Mr Dog quickly rolled and got back to his paws – only for the bloodhound and the harrier to hare up and knock him down again. Mr Dog fell, winded, barking in warning, but the other dogs yapped louder.

'No!' Lizzie said sternly – leaving Hog in the cage up in the tree, she quickly jumped between Mr Dog and the hounds. 'Four against one isn't fair, is it? Where are your owners? Get off with you.'

But the hounds did not back down. 'She can't keep you safe from us,' Dandy yapped. 'Nobody can!'

But Mr Dog wasn't looking at the blustering basset any more. His eyes were fixed on Hog, who'd now crept out of the cage . . . and, perhaps

inspired by Maura's talk of climbing hedgehogs,

was starting to wriggle up the tree branch!

Lizzie hadn't noticed her prickly escaping

prisoner, trying to keep eye contact with Dandy,

the leader of the pack. 'You're as stubborn as

your owner, aren't you? And almost as annoying!'

At first, Mr Dog thought that Hog was just scared and trying to escape. Then he realised that Hog was in fact bravely balancing on the branch right above the threatening hounds, even while Lizzie tried to calm them down . . .

'No, Hog!' Mr Dog woofed.

But he was too late. Suddenly, Hog jumped!

'GERONIMOOOO!'

Curling into a ball, Hog landed on Dandy's head, his prickles poking between the basset's floppy ears. Dandy yelped and jumped in surprise, as Hog bounced off – and biffed the barking bloodhound on the bonce too. As he rebounded, Hog hit the harrier's head as well! With perfect timing, Mr Dog dashed forward, barged the ridgeback aside and caught Hog neatly in his jaws like a spiky ball.

Then he retreated behind Lizzie. He needn't have worried, though. Yelping in surprise and confusion, the hounds had hightailed it away, with Dandy fleeing after them through the woods.

'Not so scary after all, were they?' said Hog happily.

'Dandy's bark was worse than his bite, as we dogs say.' Mr Dog put the hedgie down and gave his nose a fond nuzzle. 'You were amazing, Hog! You stopped that situation before it could get nasty.'

'You've helped me so much,' said Hog. 'I wanted to help you too.'

Lizzie was staring down at Mr Dog and Hog in wonder. 'You two are quite the double act, aren't you?'

112

Mr Dog sat politely and, again, offered a paw.

'I have the strangest feeling that you were trying to help this little guy all along, not hurt him. Which makes you all right with me.' Lizzie bent down and carefully picked up Hog. 'I'm going to take you home and put you in a nice cosy carry-case. I'll look after you until I've caught enough hedgies to take back to the mainland again, and then you'll start a safer, happier life . . .'

Mr Dog lay down on his side

and gave a happy sigh. 'That IS good news.'

'But what about all the other poor hedgehogs?'
said Maura, popping up again from the leaves.
'For every one that Lizzie saves, Moaning Minnie
Maitland deals with two more. It's not fair!'

No, it's not, thought Mr Dog. *But whatever can
be done about it now?*

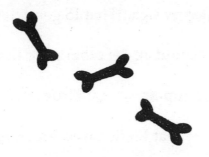

Chapter Ten

A NEW START

Mr Dog followed Lizzie back to her farmhouse. It turned out that she fed her rescued hedgies dog food, and plenty of it! She put out bowls for both her new guests in one of the outbuildings.

'Delicious!' Hog declared, munching on kibble

inside his nice, cosy carry-case.

'I'm glad to hear it.' Mr Dog licked his chops
as he finished his own meal. 'Better than wader
eggs?'

Hog licked his little food dish. 'A hundred
times better, I bet!'

'I agree,' came a little squeak from behind him.

'Me too,' came another.

'I recognise those voices,' Hog gasped. 'Sprackle! Tucker! My little hedgie friends!'

'Really?' Mr Dog gave his biggest doggy grin and stood on his back legs to greet the little hedgehogs, each in a pet crate. 'Hog was afraid he'd lost you.'

'It was a human giant called Jed who found us,' said Sprackle. 'He said we would be checked to be sure we're healthy, then taken to a place called Mainland to begin a better life.'

'Mainland,' Hog said dreamily. 'That's where the first hedgehogs came from, a thousand seasons past.'

'Wow!' Tucker was impressed. 'You sure know a lot, Hog.'

'Jed the giant was waiting for his friend, frizzy Lizzie, to come back,' Sprackle said. 'He hoped she'd be bringing good news. Is finding Hog the good news?'

'It's the best news,' said Mr Dog. 'But I suppose Jed must've meant something else.'

'I wonder what?' said Hog.

Then the farmhouse doorbell rang.

Mr Dog trotted back to the house to see who was calling – and as Lizzie and Jed opened the door, he found it wasn't good news at all. Mrs Maitland had come to call, and she didn't look

pleased. Dandy, back on his lead, growled crossly.

'That no-good stray!' Mrs Maitland pointed at Mr Dog. 'What's he doing here?'

'He's staying with me for a while, until I take him back to the mainland,' said Lizzie. 'Like my hedgies, he can start another life there.'

I'm rather fond of the one I have, thought Mr Dog. *But you're very sweet to think of me!*

'That dog's been out worrying sheep,' said Mrs Maitland. 'Ought to be locked up.'

Jed folded his arms. 'What about your Dandy? I heard Farmer Donaldson say he gave a whole herd of cattle a fright, running off the lead with his friends.'

'They gave me a scare too,' Lizzie added. 'Still,
I do hope that all those hounds have been safely
recovered?'

'Yes.' Mrs Maitland harrumphed. 'I was out
all day searching for Dandy. Found him and the
others skulking in the woods near here and got
them all in my van. Something had spooked
them.'

Lizzie winked at Mr Dog.
'I can't imagine what.'

Mr Dog grinned.
'Beware of low-flying
hedgies,' he woofed,
and Dandy cringed.

Mrs Maitland stepped up to Lizzie. 'I'm here because I believe that you and Jed turned that stray dog loose on purpose to sabotage our hunt,' she went on. 'What do you say to that, hmm?'

'It's not true,' Lizzie said.

Jed nodded. 'We would never do such a thing, because the poor thing could've been hurt – just like those hedgehogs you find.'

Lizzie smiled. 'Still, the good news is, the Isle of Evan's hedgehogs are finally safe from your horrible hunts, Mrs Maitland. Because, you see, I didn't just go to the mainland to release our rescued hedgies. I invited members of the Scottish Nature Trust along, to see what we're doing.'

'Aye, she did,' said Jed, waving a piece of paper. 'And they were so impressed, they've just confirmed that they're banning all hedgehog hunts on the Isle of Evan. They want to help fund our "catch-with-kindness" scheme instead.'

Mrs Maitland had gone very pale. '*Ban?*' she spluttered. 'Fund *you?*'

'Hurray!' Mr Dog threw back his head and howled with happiness.

Dandy dropped to the floor, whining. 'Not fair!'

'It's good news for sure,' Mr Dog agreed. 'And, goodbye!' He scampered away to tell Hog and the other hedgies. They couldn't believe their little ears!

'No more hunts?' said Hog, his black eyes wide with wonder. 'A new start for all of us?'

'Well, I don't suppose it's possible to move *all* of the hedgehogs here back to the mainland,' said Mr Dog. 'But hopefully they can find the right balance so that the island's wildlife will live together in harmony. I can't wait to slip out and share the news with Maura!'

'How kind you are,' said Hog happily. 'Will you come back after, Mr Dog?'

'Of course, for a while,' he wuffed. 'We'll all take the ferryboat back to the mainland and I can see you settled into your new lives before carrying on my way.'

'Thank you.' Hog pressed his little nose through the bars in his carry-case and Mr Dog pushed his big nose up against it. 'I never would have got here without you.'

'Well, I couldn't leave you behind, could I?' Mr Dog grinned. 'After all, it's not every day that I meet a talking hedge . . . and practically *never* that I meet a hedge called Hog!'

Notes from the Author

There's something special and different about hedgehogs. With their sharp, prickly coats, beady eyes and little snouts they might not look that beautiful – and they are very shy – but there is nothing like them anywhere else in Britain. I love watching the way they snuffle for food or curl into a ball if they think they are in danger. And I still wait up at night sometimes, watching very quietly, hoping one will appear in my London garden (even though it never has!).

Hedgehogs live in both the town and the country and really don't usually need much more than the right food and somewhere dark and quiet to hide. But sometimes in this busy human world this isn't easy, so occasionally we just have to give them a bit of help. Remember that one might be living in a pile of dead leaves or under a bush or compost heap, so be careful if you disturb them. If you have a hedgehog nearby, think about whether you might leave out a little extra food when it's time for them to get ready to hibernate for the winter or when they have just woken up in the spring. They will happily eat dog food or cat food and like water (not milk) to drink. And if anyone is lighting a bonfire, ask them to check for hedgehogs first!

Hedgehogs are nocturnal animals so they only usually go out at night. If you see one during the day, it might have a problem. If you find a hedgehog in daylight and it looks lost, don't touch it but ring your local hedgehog rescue centre or a hedgehog charity instead for advice. Hedgehogs really need our friendship – even if they can't tell us so.

Read on for a sneak peek of
Mr Dog's next adventure,

MR DOG
AND THE FARAWAY FOX

Chapter One

A CRY IN THE NIGHT

It was late in the city. The roads were quiet and the house windows were dark. But not all animals went to bed just because humans did! Nocturnal creatures still roamed the streets and gardens . . .

An eerie sound, like a howling scream, rose up into the starry springtime blackness of the sky.

Mr Dog jumped awake, his dark eyes wide

under their bushy brows. He was a raggedy mutt, with dark scruffy fur, a big black nose and front paws as white as his muzzle. 'What a curious noise,' he said to himself, stretching with a yawn. 'I wonder what it was?'

The short, sad, yowling cry came again. Mr Dog pit-patted across the kitchen to the back door, stuck his head out through the catflap and raised an ear. He was trying to trace the lonely sound. But the night was quiet again, just the grumble of a passing car in a nearby road, so he went back inside.

Mr Dog didn't often stay in cities. A travelling dog by nature, he preferred fresh air, fields and forests. If he chose to stay with a pet owner it was usually in a sleepy town or small-time village. But a little while ago he had stepped on a thorn and his paw had grown sore. He'd limped into town in search of help.

Luckily, a kind, animal-loving lady called Minnah had found him and taken him home. She'd pulled out the thorn with tweezers, given him a good bath and even washed the red-and-white spotted hanky that served as his collar! Her friend was a vet who had checked Mr Dog's paw, and luckily the only treatment needed was to soak it in a special bath for ten minutes, twice a day.

'It's really feeling much better already,' thought Mr Dog, waggling his paw. 'And how sweet and clean I smell! I may have to change my name to Lord Dog…' He stood on his back paws and tried to look as posh as possible. 'Hmm, perhaps even *Sir* Dog?'

'Sir Silly Dog!' someone giggled from a pet-carrier on the kitchen floor.

'Silly? I'm being serious.' Mr Dog beamed at the tortoise inside the carrier. 'Or *sir*-ious, at least.

How are you feeling, Shelly?'

Shelly pushed out his little scaly head. 'I'm feeling glad to have such a noble neighbour!' he said. Shelly was a fifteen-year-old Horsfield tortoise with a richly patterned shell and a sense of fun that was missing in many tortoises. 'I just really hope that someone finds poor old Crawly soon.'

'So do I,' Mr Dog agreed sadly. Crawly was another tortoise who for years had lived with Shelly in a nearby garden. Then, two days ago, Crawly had gone missing. There was no sign of forced entry to the garden. No one knew what had happened. Since the tortoises' owners had to go away for a few days, they'd asked Minnah to look after Crawly in case something happened to him too.

'One minute Crawly was there beneath a

hedge,' Shelly said, not for the first time, 'and the next minute . . . he was gone.' Shelly's head slowly shrank back inside his shell. 'It all happened so fast.'

'Don't lose hope.' Mr Dog put his nose to the side of the carry-case and snuffled Shelly's shell. 'Crawly might still show up, you know . . .' Suddenly he heard the creak of a floorboard. The kitchen light flicked on and Minnah came into the room.

'Hello, boy,' she yawned, patting his head. Mr Dog woofed softly in greeting and wagged his brushy tail.

'That screaming fox woke you up too, did it?' said Minnah, filling the kettle. 'What a racket, calling out like that...'

'A fox!' Shelly shivered in his shell – though, of course, Minnah couldn't hear a word he said.

'I never knew that a fox could make a sound like that.'

'Nor me,' Mr Dog agreed. 'Minnah certainly taught us something tonight.'

Shelly's dark eyes twinkled. 'You mean . . . she "*tortoise*" something!'

Mr Dog rolled on to his back and wriggled in amusement. Shelly beamed.

Minnah made herself a cup of tea, fed Mr Dog a biscuit and then switched out the light and went back up to bed.

Mr Dog had just settled himself back in his basket when the eerie fox cry sounded again.

'I don't like the thought of a fox being so close by,' Shelly confessed. 'My owner said it could've been a fox who took Crawly from the garden.'

'I hope not,' said Mr Dog, who was a friend to all animals and never one to judge. 'Dogs and foxes tend to avoid each other, so I haven't really met one before . . .'

After a while, Shelly fell asleep. But Mr Dog's ears jumped as the strange howl sounded once more from outside.

I wonder why that fox is calling? thought Mr Dog. *Perhaps it's in trouble. Maybe I can help?* Limping just a little, Mr Dog padded over to the catflap and squeezed through it. *At the very least, I can ask him to keep the noise down so he doesn't disturb the neighbours . . .*

The catflap opened on to a side alley: one way led to the main street, the other to a quiet lane that backed on to a row of garages. The night was cool and Mr Dog's nose twitched with the city's scents. The houses were dark but the streetlamps cast bright orange patches over the pavements. Somewhere distant, gulls gave their rowdy cries and a clock struck three. Mr Dog felt happy. How nice it was to be outside again!

His nose twitched with a strong, musky smell from the fir trees that lined someone's garden. *That fox has marked this territory*, thought Mr Dog. *A boy fox, unless I'm very much mistaken. He must be close by . . .*

Then Mr Dog caught another smell.

The smell of a tortoise!

Quickly he pushed his head through the fir trees – and couldn't believe his eyes.

A small and scrappy red fox was sitting happily in the garden – holding a tortoise in its jaws!